Martin Rust

Optimize the Moment

From War Zones to Boardrooms: Optimize the Moment
When Strategic Planning Fails

©2023 Martin Rust

Purple Works Press
41 Avenida Fernando Luis Ribas #449
Utuado, Puerto Rico 00641
www.purpleworkspress.com

ISBN: eBook 979-8-9902232-0-2

ISBN: Paperback 979-8-9902232-3-3

ISBN: Hardcover 979-8-9902232-1-9

First edition: March 2024

Printed in the USA

Table of Contents

Reviews

I have known Martin professionally for a number of years and now I understand why he follows the consistent framework in his Professional Consulting and is successful in doing so. Very few individuals come with the diversity of experience, cultural understanding, and firsthand leadership experience that has hardened the Optimize the Moment *business model and journey through the "Mission." I found myself emotionally reflecting on past and present approaches that helped me ponder my leadership style, especially with the closing section of profound questions designed to operationalize each chapter's learning. I will use this book as a manual going forward to articulate, communicate, plan, execute, review, and adjust the Mission. This is a must read for new and seasoned leaders alike.*

Terry Nemeth, Senior Leader & Management Consultant, Strategy Corp

Having read Optimize the Moment *helped me reframe my thinking. Throughout my life I have been fortunate to have worked for small entities right up through Fortune 100 companies, and it is with this lens that I read* Optimize the Moment. Optimize the Moment *helped me to alter the way I look at things; not everything is a nail, with me thinking like a hammer. Martin will take you down several paths, all of which are worth following to the end as they are brought together in very insightful ways. I have just recently started an advisory business, and learning from* Optimize the Moment *and the way Martin takes you through the experiences that shaped his world will be instrumental in the success of my new venture.*

I tend to read and listen to many books. I put Optimize the Moment *right up beside my collection of favorites including works by Gladwell, Blount, Grant, Purja, and McRaven.*

Dave McAllister, Senior Advisor, Vincita

The book pulled me in immediately and spoke to me as it said things that I had always hoped were true about how major world-impacting decisions were being made. On the outside, we often see/hear about all of the bad outcomes, but it was great to be a fly on the wall to see that there really are smart people on the inside working hard to do the right thing. I am a sucker for a good story about geo-politics, so having the book start out that way was definitely a bonus!

I found the subtitle "when strategic planning fails" quite humorous as I recall in the early days of my career that organizations had an intense focus on creating "5-Year Plans" - big binders of facts and figures and goals (in reality, dreams). Folks always poked fun at the documents they were creating, knowing full well that they were not even worth the paper they were being printed on. Alas, every year there was a review/refresh cycle, and the directors would go off to some meeting with their department's "FIVE-YEAR PLAN" binder tucked under their arm...sigh.

The most resounding takeaway for me was the focus on people and empathy, something that is sorely missing these days in both our political and business environments. It's strange and unnerving that this concept has to be spelled out since companies / organizations / governments / countries are composed of actual humans to serve human needs. Many books/articles I have read talk only of "resources," so it is refreshing to see that people are the cornerstone to the Optimize the Moment *process.*

The book also gave me hope about my personal career struggles/concerns because it put my problems into a larger context: I am not going through the worst day of my life where I have lost my home, family, livelihood, all the while battling physical and/or emotional injury. If someone going through that level of crisis can pull themselves together, place one foot in front of the other, and rebuild and prosper, so can I!

I found the book to be transformative as it aligned with components of the thought process I use to work through problems, but provided me with a more comprehensive, organized (and successful) framework to facilitate actual execution. I wish I had access to this framework earlier in my career; I would have saved myself from a number of head whacks as a result of trial and error -- so many errors... A more specific example: I can get a bit mired in analyzing risk and have to catch myself before I fall too far down the rabbit hole. Going forward, I can see myself adopting the "optimize the moment" process to step through my decision-making and project execution. It's always great to have a checklist to follow to keep you on the path.

I regularly consider people in the business decisions that I make, but the book has taught me that I have room for improvement. I now realize that I am not as empathetic as I could (and should be). Even though I have been successfully completing my missions, the outcomes could be more impressive / impactful if I included more empathy in my decision-making processes.

Michael Barrow, Chief Technology Officer, Titanium Forest

Martin Rust upends the traditional corporate approach to strategic planning and forecasting. We no longer live in the kind of predictable world that makes this approach possible. Rust's experience demonstrates what we all know: that geopolitical, environmental, and economic conflict and upheaval aren't anomalies, they are the new norm. Therefore, strategic planning exercises that rely on status quo conditions are doomed to fail. By optimizing the moment, defining the mission, truly listening to key stakeholders, embracing chaos, and abandoning preconceived notions, we move the organizations of today into a state of resiliency, agility, and ultimately success. Optimize The Moment *shows us how.*

Jacki Christopher, Director, National Build-to-Suit Development at Ryan Companies U.S

Martin Rust's new book, From War Zones to Boardrooms: Optimize the Moment When Strategic Planning Fails, *is both eye-opening and incredibly informative. He has performed what is really an astonishing trick, which is to distill his experiences in conflict zones and other highly stressed environments into potent life and leadership lessons that can be translated into the corporate environment. He also makes a compelling case that companies should emphasize their values over their profits, as a way to stay relevant and preserve their integrity, and increase their chances of survival in the long run.*

In his discussions of the Optimize the Moment *concept, Martin provides clear and illuminating explanations of how corporate leaders can transform their company's performance in vital areas such as problem-solving, decision-making, contingency planning, personnel management, and long-term goal setting. Despite Martin's humble approach, there is true wisdom here, and if I'd had the chance to read this book and absorb its insights when I was still working in the corporate world, I might very well have stayed. Martin's vast range of experiences make him the perfect messenger to reveal why optimizing the moment will work where strategic planning so often fails, since he has been living this truth for more than two decades.*

Nathan Falde, Freelance Writer and Editor

From War Zones to Boardrooms: Optimize the Moment When Strategic Planning Fails *by Martin Rust offers a compelling exploration of strategic decision-making in dynamic and uncertain environments. Divided into two sections, the book provides insights gleaned from the author's rich experiences in advising corporations through crises and disruptions.*

Section 1: "Strategic Plans Don't Work"

In this section, Martin Rust shares personal anecdotes and reflections on his journey from early career experiences to advising renowned corporations in boardrooms. By highlighting the limitations of traditional strategic planning approaches that are hatched at a Corporate level and targeted to appease board members, he critiques the conventional campaigns showing how they fail at addressing the complex challenges faced by employees at the front line who must implement them. Drawing on firsthand experiences, Martin Rust offers valuable insights into the shortcomings of traditional strategic planning processes and on the need for a new paradigm in corporate decision-making.

Section 2: "Optimize the Moment: A New Approach"

In the second section, Martin Rust introduces a fresh perspective on strategic decision-making, emphasizing the importance of adaptability and agility in turbulent environments. Drawing on his vantage point of observing diverse organizations in various contexts, the author outlines a new approach that prioritizes responsiveness, innovation, and resilience. Using practical examples from current events, he elucidates why each step in this approach is critical for navigating uncertainty and seizing opportunities in times of crisis.

Key Themes:

Adaptive Leadership: Martin Rust emphasizes the importance of adaptive leadership in guiding organizations through times of crisis and uncertainty. Drawing parallels between corporate executives and military commanders, he explores the qualities and strategies that enable leaders to pivot quickly, reassess priorities, and mobilize resources effectively.

Decision-Making Under Pressure: The book delves into the psychology of decision-making under pressure, highlighting the cognitive biases and pitfalls that can undermine strategic thinking. He posits that those on the front line need agility, adaptability, and the ability to make informed decisions in the face of uncertainty.

Resilience and Innovation: Martin Rust argues that resilience and innovation are essential for thriving in volatile environments. By fostering a culture of experimentation, learning, and adaptation, organizations can turn setbacks into opportunities for growth and transformation.

Collaborative Networks: The book explores the power of collaborative networks and partnerships in enhancing organizational agility and resilience. From Consultants to alliances between diverse stakeholders he encourages companies to facilitate information sharing, resource mobilization, and collective problem-solving in complex, fast-moving environments.

John Mee, Business Development, Mee Industries

For my father, Malcolm Rust, who has shown me what it means to live a life of service, for a cause greater than self, and to truly accept people for who they are, where they are, and above all, to never miss a moment to learn from others.

Love you, Dad.

Foreword

In 2008, destiny intervened when Martin offered me an opportunity to work with him in Iraq. Little did I know that a simple invitation for a Skype call with someone I had never met would lead to a transformative experience that would forever alter the course of my professional life and a lifelong friendship. I owe Martin a profound debt of gratitude for recognizing potential in me that I never thought I had, and for taking a chance on me during a pivotal and wobbly moment in my career.

At the time, I was a late twenty-something politico working in Ottawa at the Department of Foreign Affairs (as it was then called) as the Parliamentary Affairs and Communications Director for a prominent cabinet minister. I loved the travel, the cut and thrust of the politics, and even more, I loved being in the room and offering advice on major policy and political decisions of the day. To be blunt, it was a pretty cool job but paid horribly. Worse, I suffered from youthful impatience as it was clear that further advancement at that time was not in the cards. I needed a change and had to leave – but to do what? Enter Martin.

It all started in March 2008 when a close mutual friend connected Martin to me under the pretense that I needed career and coaching advice. Given that Martin was based in Iraq, I set up the Skype at an ungodly hour to accommodate his schedule. I did not view our discussion as a potential job interview because there was no way in hell that I was ever going to consider moving to a warzone. As far as I was concerned, the call was to expand my network and get pointers on improving my resume for international opportunities.

I would eventually learn that before the call, Martin had different ideas. Whatever our mutual friend said to Martin, resulted in him having several conversations about me with others even before our call. By the time I was on the call with him, I didn't stand a chance as he employed his consultative process on me that had been honed through years of experience. He prodded me to confront my deepest career and personal motivations. He didn't pontificate, rather he posed questions that were, at times, discomforting, compelling me to really look beyond superficial goals and question my readiness to take risks.

In all my life, no one had done this before with or to me. Since it was literally the first time we had ever spoken, I was a little taken aback, asking myself, "who the hell is this guy?" But he was making me think differently than I had before. Two hours into the call, I had acknowledged that my career thus far was a façade to impress others. I wanted depth. I wanted substance. Martin pushed me on what it meant to have an impact and whether I was willing to take a risk. Two weeks later, I was on a plane to Kurdistan in northern Iraq.

Unless someone has lived in a warzone, it is truly impossible to describe it. The sounds, the smells, the visuals, the camaraderie, the crushing and sinking feeling you get when a rocket hits or a bomb explodes, the loss – all play on the senses and emotions. The environment in which we lived, especially in Baghdad, was intense, fast paced, and dangerous. Martin and I were part of any amazing team of expatriates and Iraqi nationals who were dedicated to our mission of nurturing democracy in Iraq while we lived our unusual lives in captivity. We travelled in armoured vehicles in heavily armed convoys. We took different routes every day to ensure that no one learned our patterns. We had professional teams of bodyguards, all ex-special forces, who protected us 24/7 within our walled compounds or while traveling throughout the country. We took specialised weapons and hostile environment training in case we were attacked or kidnapped. Within our t-walled compounds we slept surrounded by sandbags within a 20-second run of bomb shelters.

I look back now and recognize that we lived, worked, and traveled through some superbly dangerous parts of Iraq to do our job and while doing so, survived several close calls (very close calls). I can say with the benefit of hindsight, those experiences changed us as people, but the work we were doing was impactful, and even when there was loss, we loved every minute of what we did. We took the risks we took because the work we were doing was critical to the future success of Iraq's nascent democracy. Our work also supported the efforts of other government agencies of our allied forces, as we helped them to understand who the decision-makers were in a new Iraq.

Some might question the wisdom of the U.S. invasion of Iraq; however, at the point in time we were deployed, it was long after the invasion had happened. When we were on the ground, an intense insurgency was in full swing amongst the various sectarian groups that nearly brought Iraq to the brink of civil war. Bombings and attacks on convoys were a daily occurrence. The insurgency resulted in the infamous "surge" where the U.S. increased troop levels dramatically. That brought physical safety but also made our job a little more difficult.

What was our job? Well – our job was our mission, and our mission was to calm things down amongst the members of the newly formed and elected parliament. We had to get those new elected officials into a headspace of sharing power, establishing democratic systems for self-government, and ensuring the diverse sectarian, ethnic and geographic interests represented in the parliament had a forum for dialogue to resolve their issues in a post-Saddam era without resorting to war. It was an intense mission.

The governance and oversight team that Martin led was one of three programs under the auspices of the National Democratic Institute (NDI), which was chaired at the time by the former Secretary of State, Madeleine Albright. NDI was tasked by the U.S. State Department to bring together global experts to deliver a three-part program: first, to develop civil society organizations like chambers of commerce, student unions, veteran's groups, women's rights groups, et. cetera; second, to form, build and develop a political party system that would feed into the democratic process; and, third, to advise, guide, and support the Iraqi parliament.

The Iraqi Parliament, known as the Council of Representatives, was a boiling cauldron that represented every problem facing Iraq, from sectarianism, historical grievances, corruption, seizures of power and assets, refusal to acknowledge opponents, and ethnic strife – all of which was mixed with resentment toward the Americans for the invasion (and a realization that nothing would ever be the same). Our job was to jump into this boiling cauldron and engage every member of parliament as well as their advisors, to get them to work together to build a functioning parliamentary institution. It was kind of like living in a university PoliSci 101 and International Relations class all at once. The individual stories are at times hilarious and at other times harrowing or frightening.

In some instances, there were Iraqi leaders who just refused to meet with us because in their minds we were agents of their occupiers. Martin and I would not accept that rejection because it meant failure of our mission. Our job was to engage. We knew it would take time. We respectfully pushed our agenda but did so cautiously as some of those who had rejected us were not only powerful political actors but also warlords of armed militia groups. So, we treaded carefully.

Our approach was one that is common in the Middle East, that of "a thousand cups of tea." It means we bided our time; we were always respectful; and, when we could not engage certain leaders directly, we did so indirectly by engaging those within their orbit who might have influence and would vouch that we were not a threat nor trying to impose specific outcomes. Let's just say, it was no easy task. Progress was measured in millimeters.

Our secret weapon was Martin's consultative process. We built trust through listening and delivering on promises, ultimately unlocking deeper insights into the motivations of key political leaders and those within their inner circles. Our ability to discern the power dynamics within the parliament and even those hidden behind the scenes allowed us to influence change subtly yet effectively. In essence, we ran a human intelligence gathering exercise where we gained trust not only through presence but by delivering on specific things asked of us. Predictably, as guarded actors opened up, we gained more access and thus were able to delve deeper into the true aims of certain political leaders, while laying bare how said aims might conflict with those of another. The net result was that we got movement on key objectives of our mission.

For instance, after months upon months of stalemate, we actually helped bring the Iraqis together to develop a comprehensive legislative process for passing and enacting laws. It may sound silly, but the various actors so distrusted one another, they could not even agree on a process to pass a law. Once that was achieved, we worked hand-in-glove with the very diverse Iraqi Finance Committee of Parliament to establish a national budget planning and consultation process to shape the country's national budget. That process is still used to this day. We also led very tough negotiations and mediations that resulted in power sharing deals between the political wings of various militia groups, determining who would get what positions in the parliament and who would oversee which levers of power (providing clarity to the country about who was in charge of what).

On the technical side, we helped establish the literal rules of parliament, and we brought the Speaker's Office and the Executive Branch together to establish a process where members of parliament could demand ministers answer questions about their actions and hold them accountable for decisions (which, in a country with a history where challenging the government used to result in one's death, was not an easy change to inspire). This led to more and more effective governance and oversight, including an anti-corruption commission that still works hard today to shed light on wrongdoing. The system and structures were by no means perfect, but comparing where Iraq was before we started, vis-à-vis their parliamentary system, to where they were after demonstrated a significant move in the right direction.

The experiences Martin and I had together, and that of our entire team made us very proud. But it also made us very pragmatic about life and people. I learned from Martin that the most effective advisors are those who listen more than they speak. I also learned that the best advice is often given posed as a question so that the person being advised hears the answer coming from themselves. This is the essence of the consultative process, which was the hallmark of Martin's approach with the Iraqis and with his own team. As it is said, our job was not to be a sage on the stage, but rather a guide by the side.

After I finished in Iraq, I came back to Canada a changed man. I finished the law degree that I had put on hold years before and finally became a lawyer. My practice evolved into a mix of international and domestic corporate and commercial law as well as litigation. The consultative approach is central to how I practice law and how I engage with my clients and opposing Counsel. Yes, some clients just want black-letter-law advice; however, I find most of my clients now come to me with complex problems that don't necessarily require the involvement of a lawyer. Rather, they are seeking independent gut-check advice, smart dialogue, and wargaming solutions. The desired outcome is the first step, and then we work backwards to assess what is involved to get to that outcome. Or we discuss whether the initial outcome was the right one in the first place.

To this day, I can say without equivocation that the nearly three years I lived and worked in Iraq reshaped every aspect of my life. Living in a warzone, you see both the best and the worst of humanity. Both Martin and I saw things that we cannot unsee and experienced things we wish we hadn't. But we have persevered and relied upon each other to navigate down times. We have both learned that in life you must have a healthy and, at times, macabre sense of humour. Doubly important is the ability to laugh at yourself, especially in front of others, as it makes you human.

When Martin asked me to write the foreword to this book it gave me a chance to go back and review his tremendous career and record of success. It is worth taking a moment to talk about his incredible experience and skill set.

Early in his career, as I did, Martin got his start in politics serving as a political adviser to Canada's Minister of Finance. This gave him tremendous insight into the financial mechanisms that impact the

Government of Canada's fiscal framework. After government, he became a senior financial advisor with Merrill Lynch, which went on to become CIBC World Markets. He was then recruited to become Vice President of a large private wealth management company servicing high-net-worth individuals, leading to his appointment as CEO of WealthFunds SPC in Jakarta, Indonesia.

That corporate experience was rewarding, and Martin built a sound nest egg. But he wanted to give back outside the corporate world. He saw an opportunity to move into the international non-governmental organizations sector and to support the tremendous work of both the National Democratic Institute and the International Republican Institute. If you are not familiar with these organizations, look them up. They have done some tremendous work in advancing democracy and governance around the world and have a proven track record of success. When Martin joined, his experience was put to good use and he spent years advising the senior-most officials and political leaders in Algeria, Jordan, Pakistan, Tunisia, Ukraine, and, of course, in Iraq.

While Martin still does international non-governmental work on an ad hoc basis, when Martin returned to Canada 2009/2010, he was tapped to run a major public affairs firm in Ottawa. From there, he moved on to become a senior advisor at one of Canada's top corporate and government relations strategy firms. His clients now include some of North America's largest and most savvy corporations. He now advises C-Suite executives on emerging issues and global risk, and he continues to use his consultative approach to challenge leaders to think differently. Since Martin believes in living a balanced life, in addition to being a dad to two (now adult) kids he has allowed his lifelong love and passion for horses to come to life. A lifelong rider, he is a leader in the Ottawa Hunt Club, competes in horse jumping and owns a spectacular horse farm and stable on the outskirts of Ottawa.

Optimize the Moment

As you read Optimize the Moment, you can rest assured that the points Martin makes are rooted in real experiences that most wouldn't have in a lifetime. I have appreciated the thoughtful approach he has taken to challenge corporate leaders to focus on and articulate clear missions and action plans. Note, I did not say 'mission statements,' I said missions. Martin expands more in the book on this difference, but I can assure you, having worked with him in warzones, understanding the difference between the two is a key driver of success or failure. You will read that lofty and nebulous mission statements can help people in organizations look in the same direction, but it will be missions with specific and required goal that will guide the people you lead to success.

Enjoy the read.

Jeffrey J. Kroeker, B.A. (Hons.), J.D.

Lawyer, Partner of Massey LLP

Introduction

As the world continues to change at a breakneck pace, the boundaries between conflict and commerce often blur, compelling us to adapt and learn continuously. In this ever-shifting landscape, my own path has led me through myriad fascinating experiences, many of which are rather unconventional.

I've witnessed the intensity of conflict, worked in post-conflict zones, and learned how to navigate the intricacies of boardrooms. My journey has been less about directing and more about discovering and learning, and sharing insights picked up from these diverse environments.

This book is not a manual written by someone claiming to have all the answers. It is a collection of observations and experiences that highlight the resilience and adaptability of the human spirit under extreme pressure. As I share these stories, my aim is not to present myself as an expert with perfect solutions, but as someone who has had the privilege of being on the scene during many pivotal moments, when tough choices were made and good results were achieved. These experiences have afforded me a unique perspective on leadership and decision-making, which can perhaps be beneficial to you (just as my reflections on these experiences have been beneficial to me).

My narrative is just one part of a larger story. More than anything, this book celebrates the courage and wisdom of people I've encountered during my journey. Each chapter is an homage to the unsung heroes whose decisions have shaped our world in positive but often unseen ways.

I call my book *From War Zones to Boardrooms: Optimize the Moment When Strategic Planning Fails* because I have every intention of provoking a discussion about how decisions are made, one that can potentially go deep enough to disrupt how businesses are run. I hope to demonstrate that strategic planning, although commonplace in government, as well as in small and large companies alike, doesn't really work. Strategic plans, while valuable at the highest level, don't help leaders make decisions on the ground or in the field, during those crucial moments or in those split seconds when they count the most. This is especially true in the turbulent times in which we live.

My 25-year career has taken me to Iraq, Ukraine, Algeria, Kurdistan, Indonesia, Pakistan, and Jordan. From my collective experiences in these remarkable places, I constructed the foundation of my consulting approach, which I call Optimize the Moment™.

Optimize the Moment is all about seizing opportunities and making the most of the challenges we all face, while also understanding the power of effective communication. It can help you realize your potential for empathetic leadership, which can have true transformative power in just about any situation. The principles behind Optimize the Moment are not rigid but flexible, meaning they can be adapted and molded to fit your own unique circumstances.

As you turn these pages, I invite you to reflect on and question everything you read, and even challenge the ideas presented. This book is as much about your journey of discovery as it is about mine.

My professional history is rather unusual. When I was first starting out over a quarter of a century ago, I didn't dream that one day I'd be acting as an advisor to Fortune 100 companies and governments. I can't say I even sought that role or knew much about the concept of the "corporate consigliere."

I've worked in countries many wouldn't dare visit, from war-torn regions to countries in crisis. Instead of just reading reports in a comfortable office, I've worked in conflict zones and post-conflict zones, listening to people's stories, and learning to understand the challenges they've faced. My first-hand experience has taught me the importance of making genuine human connections, showing me how understanding and compassion can help solve even the toughest and most complicated problems. Through my immersions in these intense environments, I've gained a vantage point that has allowed me to see what works well and what doesn't, which is incredibly valuable and also quite humbling, since the truth will often not conform to our expectations.

I've been surrounded by people in dire circumstances who've literally lost everything, including their homes and their families, frequently while dealing with severe, life-altering injuries. And yet, they didn't retreat into a corner and surrender. They decided instead to find and pursue a purpose, many times leading others who were doing the same. I have witnessed extreme acts of courage and bravery, inspiring a type of decision-making that we can all study and learn from.

In many ways, this book is a tribute to those individuals who along the way have optimized those moments and made brave decisions. This book is not primarily my story, but theirs, and I will be forever grateful for the examples they've set.

Optimize the Moment is not fancy corporate jargon, but a simple concept that can help you formulate achievable goals, based on some profound but fully comprehensible ideas. It can show you how to make the best of every situation, without overthinking and over-planning. It will help you recognize those moments in life where your decisions can have a real impact on the future, and, I hope, it will encourage you to act in these situations with intention and without deliberation.

And it can empower groups as well as individuals. Optimize the Moment emphasizes the importance of building a solid team and understanding that each member's contributions are key. Clear communication is essential, as everyone should understand the mission and their role in it. I consider my approach empathy-based and purpose-driven because it prioritizes each person's role in the plan over the plan itself (which in the end actually makes the plan easier to implement).

There is something I tell my clients that has rung true for many millennia: "Most problems in life are the result of poor communication. We all communicate every day, and yet, it is something we rarely do well. Effective communication does not happen by default nor is it measured by quantity; excellent communication is simple and clear."

Overcoming barriers to communication is essential for successful interactions. Utilizing clear, jargon-free language is vital, as company- and industry-specific terminology can easily hinder clear communication.

Effective communication, or common understanding, demands a carefully crafted narrative that resonates with decision-makers and can be easily repeated across various levels. The manner of delivery – be it through email, phone, or direct contact – and consistency in tone and language are equally important.

The contexts within which communication occurs will vary, and achieving effective communication when interacting with government officials or heads of Fortune 100 companies will only be possible when the special challenges are understood and acknowledged.

In these rarified environments, improving communication skills requires intentional effort and practice, and is essential for achieving business objectives. Developing these skills not only resolves existing communication challenges but will also help to set your business apart, making it more influential and making you more successful in your dealings with government agencies, customers, stakeholders, and employees.

Optimize the Moment, the book as well as the concept, is for anyone striving to successfully navigate the complexities of today's rapidly changing world by making more informed and thoughtful decisions. It is not solely for corporate decision-makers, but is appropriate for everyone from business leaders of all types to individuals facing unique life challenges who wish to broaden their perspectives. This book is particularly relevant for those who are at a crossroads, whether in their professional journeys or personal lives. It's for those eager to understand the intricate dynamics of global events and for anyone interested in finding innovative paths forward in these turbulent times.

Whether you're leading a team, coping with personal challenges, or simply seeking to expand your understanding of the world, Optimize the Moment offers valuable insights to inform and enhance your decision-making process. These insights are grounded in the real-world experiences of people I've observed throughout my career, individuals who've achieved remarkable results despite being forced to act during times of crisis, or when the stakes have been at their highest.

Some of the things I'll share may seem straightforward. But within the context of working with companies and organizations over the past 25 years, every anecdote or observation forms one piece of the puzzle that is the Optimize the Moment approach.

The book is laid out in two sections.

In the first section, "Strategic Plans Don't Work," I share some of my background and explain how my experiences have shaped the perspective I hold today. I will take you through my journey from a young 30-something just making my way in the world, to sitting in the boardrooms of some of the world's most well-known corporations, advising them on their day-to-day operations, devising strategies to overcome market and supply chain disruptions, or helping them navigate geopolitical crises.

In the second section, "Optimize the Moment: A New Approach," I'll break down my methodology and explain why each step in the process is so important. My insights emerge from my experiences with various organizations, in different settings, and I have had the benefit of seeing for myself what has been successful, even in turbulent or chaotic environments.

At certain points, I provide case studies that illustrate what happens when companies cling to strategic planning, contrasting them with outcomes enjoyed by organizations that implemented the paradigm shift I have come to call Optimize the Moment.

These case studies may or may not refer to companies with whom I do business. My client list is a closely guarded secret, so you shouldn't assume my inclusion of a particular enterprise's experience implies anything about my relationship with them.

At the end of each chapter, I will pose some questions. There are no right or wrong answers, the point is simply to provoke discussion and reflection about the decision-making process. I don't profess to have all the answers myself, which is why I will never stop encouraging dialogue. My goal is to share what I have learned during my 25-year career, which you can apply to your situation as you see fit.

Before you start reading my book, I'd like to acknowledge something. I have been fortunate enough to meet many people immediately following what we would probably call "the worst day of their lives." They've been to hell and back, and that is something most of us cannot truly fathom. And yet through a variety of challenging circumstances that must have seemed to be without end, they demonstrated a will to keep putting one foot in front of the other. The more difficult things became for them, the greater their desire to succeed because they knew their efforts would lead them to a better life for their family, their community, and their country.

Their collective desire and my interactions with them are the true inspiration for Optimize the Moment. This book is for them.

And of course it is for you as well. So, are you ready to Optimize the Moment?

SECTION 1
Strategic Plans Don't Work

How the Landscape
Has Changed

All of us – from consumers to entrepreneurs and employees in businesses owned by others, plus those who represent the interests of national/federal governments – must navigate a sea of unforeseen disruptions. These disruptions impact markets, geopolitics, and the environment, each bearing the potential to profoundly reshape the landscape for organizations and for their workforce, stakeholders, and consumers. To say that we live in turbulent times is the understatement of the day.

Given this ever-evolving terrain, business leaders must come to terms with a jarring reality: traditional strategic plans are no longer satisfactory, and further, they simply don't work. Similarly, traditional decision-making tools are no longer adequate to the task at hand. To remain effective, leaders must pivot and adapt, embracing innovative approaches that can withstand the winds of change in this dynamic and unpredictable environment.

How Businesses Can Respond Under Market-Shifting Duress

More volatile and complicated situations demand next-level thinking from business leaders. The lens through which decisions are made is different, requiring new inputs and considerations.

Geopolitical upheavals halfway around the world add layers of complexity, influencing global supply chains, market access, and even how staff and suppliers at home will behave. Environmental concerns, like climate change and resource scarcity, also require fundamentally new sustainable practices that have far-reaching implications. As a consequence, traditional strategic planning needs to be reevaluated or reinvented to ensure resilience and continued success.

The working culture has experienced a profound transformation. The evolution of where and why people work has rendered many traditional workplaces and business plans obsolete. Nowadays, employees aren't driven by old-school business strategies. Instead, they're looking for missions filled with purpose, goals they can realistically achieve, and opportunities to join teams that prioritize growth and continuous learning.

Furthermore, there's an evident lack of connection in most traditional strategic plans. Their long timelines and intricate attention to detail often seem out of step with real-world scenarios, which frequently involve sudden and unanticipated developments. As a result, many employees find it hard to see where they fit into these plans. This creates a growing divide between board members, management, and the rest of the staff.

Strategic Plans Don't Work, But Don't Just Take My Word for It

There's abundant proof of the high failure rate of strategic planning. A 2022 study from Harvard Business School found that 60% of strategic initiatives just don't make the cut, producing results that are the very opposite of impressive. And get this: a jaw-dropping 95% of employees surveyed in this study could only shrug their shoulders when asked to identify or explain their company's main game plan[1]. To top it off, research by McKinsey and Company across various sectors revealed that only 30% of execs believe their current strategies are doing the trick[2].

Given what the numbers reveal, it's not surprising to learn that 72% of CEOs feared losing their jobs in 2022—and half of them held positions in companies whose gross earnings exceeded $100 million annually, according to an article published in Fortune Magazine[3].

This sentiment reflects the tumultuous business environment and the challenges CEOs face in steering their companies through uncertain times. It's a stark reminder of the need for adaptive leadership strategies, and as a corporate consultant who hears about CEO pain points every day I'm acutely aware of the necessity of evolving our leadership tactics to meet the actual requirements of today's dynamic business world.

In a January 2023 poll conducted by Gallup[4], only 32% of employees reported feeling a sense of engagement in their jobs. The low number relates to a lack of:

---

1   "4 Common Reasons Strategies Fail." Harvard Business Review, June 2022. https://hbr.org/2022/06/4-common-reasons-strategies-fail.

2   McKinsey & Company. "The State of Organizations 2023." McKinsey & Company, 2023. https://www.mckinsey.com/~/media/mckinsey/business%20functions/people%20and%20organizational%20performance/our%20insights/the%20state%20of%20organizations%202023/the-state-of-organizations-2023.pdf.

3   Majority of CEOs Anxious About Losing Jobs in 2022." Fortune. February 2, 2022. https://fortune.com/2022/02/02/majority-ceos-anxiety-losing-job-2022/.

4   Gallup. 2023. "Employee Engagement Needs to Rebound in 2023." Gallup Workplace. Accessed January 2023. https://www.gallup.com/workplace/468233/employee-engagement-needs-rebound-2023.aspx

- Connection to the mission or purpose in the company

- Clarity of expectations

- Opportunities to learn and grow

- Freedom to do what staff members do best

- Care and concern for employees' welfare

Women and younger employees felt the least connected to their company's missions, among those who knew what those missions were.

Here's the kicker: these plans are all about "strategy," but they're mostly rooted in worry rather than adjusting to developments in the real world, like what consumers are actually thinking about and focusing on right now. They might make executives feel like they've achieved something, but they often fail in the real world because they're just not in sync with what's happening on the ground. That's why most strategic plans produce mediocre results at best.

And How We Work Has Changed

Let's talk about the way we work.

Since the Covid-19 pandemic in 2020 forced us all to work from home and online, traditional work hours and productivity measurements have gone out the window. Leaders today are still wrestling with a new type of thinking that will seek a balance between productivity, work-life balance, and being able to inspire people by values and the opportunity to make a difference.

What stands out to me is the need for a business approach that's all heart, full of both purpose and empathy. It's like what global military forces call the Mission Command vibe (which I will explain in greater detail later in this chapter). It's about being clear on what you want, but not being super strict about how to get there. This way, we can quickly adapt to whatever curveballs life throws at us, and that's how we get those big wins.

Making purpose the heart and soul of a business can change everything. It helps you move with the times, connect with new trends, build trust, and make your company's mission crystal clear. And when you nail this? Employees get fired up, everyone is eager to get on board, and the positive ripple effects are felt far and wide.

Unfortunately, I've seen many companies make decisions based exclusively on fear, and it always backfires. Take Kodak, for instance.

Case Study: Kodak's Missteps Should Serve as a Valuable Lesson to Us All About Holding True to Strategic Plans

Back in 1888, Kodak founder George Eastman started something big with his invention of roll film. It was a game-changer, turning photography from a complicated procedure into a snap.

Kodak's original marketing was on point, too. "You Press the Button, We Do the Rest," their advertisements said. It was like they were ringing in a new age of simple, fun photography.

But after decades of success, the environment changed, thanks to innovations in digital photography. And when the world started going digital, Kodak got cold feet. Even though they had a digital camera prototype in the 1970s, they pulled back and tried to suppress the technology, scared it would ruin their film business.

That decision, based on fear, had dire consequences for Kodak. While Canon, Nikon and Sony rode the digital wave, Kodak got left in the dust. Their story is a harsh lesson on what happens when you don't evolve with the times.

The Moral of the Story

In the end, it's not about some grand plan. Staying "on mission" doesn't mean don't change or don't innovate. On the contrary, when an organization is "on mission," the team is focused on bringing the best ideas forward, adapting, innovating, and creating, to accomplish the mission. Organizations that create spaces where everyone feels heard, where people aren't afraid to bring ideas forward, and where the purpose is the key motivation, are the organizations that come out on top in the long run.

I have seen companies release multiple strategic plans in a single year. Often there is a new strategic plan each year, or when there is a change in leadership in the company. It is not hard to imagine why these plans end up being poorly communicated, why there is little buy-in, why people don't see themselves in the plans, and ultimately, why they don't come to fruition. As a result, the inevitable failure of such plans causes a sense of mistrust and skepticism within organizations and among stakeholders. This not only perpetuates a cycle filled with misleading information but also leads to poor decision-making.

With respect to the marketplace, many strategic plans seem out of touch. The root of the issue often lies in a lack of honesty and objectivity when formulating these strategies. This mismatch with marketplace reality can result in missed opportunities and a disconnection in market positioning, often leading to a talent drain.

Frequently, there's a glaring audience mismatch in the creation of strategic plans. They're often crafted with board members and investors in mind, sidelining the very people responsible for their execution. This misalignment diminishes the credibility of these plans, making them seem outdated and ineffective, especially when targeted at modern-day challenges.

Regardless of the size of the business, leaders should consider rethinking their approach to decision-making, moving away from traditional strategic plans toward more adaptive and agile approaches. I know from experience that this can produce a dramatic shift in results.

How Disruptions Can Dramatically Impact the Way Business is Conducted

The volatility of global markets can be affected by factors like natural disasters, tensions between nations, technological advancements, shifting consumer behaviors, and as we saw at the start of 2020, global pandemics. My experiences living and working with people in conflict and post-conflict areas over the past two decades has certainly opened my eyes to the impact of such factors (I will go into specifics about the work I did in different regions later in the book).

Geopolitical tensions between nations have risen in recent years and dominate the headlines. We hear many tragic and heartbreaking stories about events taking place halfway around the world, and this has ramifications that extend beyond immediate borders. Decision-makers are directly impacted today by the increased complexity of the world in which we live, precisely at a time when the tools at their disposal have changed and the traditional paradigms no longer apply.

How Tensions Between Two Nations Can Have Far-Reaching Impact

On October 7, 2023, a significant and dramatic event occurred in the years-long war between Israel and Palestine that caused a profound impact on both the Israeli and Palestinian communities. The day began with an attack by Hamas fighters at the Supernova festival in southern Israel, leading to the tragic loss of 364 lives and the kidnapping of 240 individuals.

This attack triggered a substantial military response from Israel, including a relentless aerial bombardment of Gaza and the deployment of hundreds of thousands of reservists. Within weeks, a ground operation in Gaza was underway.

Israel's objective was stated as the destruction of Hamas and the liberation of captives taken to Gaza. This event led to heightened tensions and a palpable shift in perceptions within Israeli society. The attack was not only a significant military and political incident, but also a deeply emotional and psychological one, affecting the collective psyche of the Israeli population.

Following the attack, there were noticeable changes in the attitudes of people worldwide toward both Israelis and Palestinians. Many Israelis who previously believed in coexistence found their views altered, seeing Hamas, and sometimes Palestinians in general, as the enemy. This shift was evident in various segments of Israeli society, impacting the attitudes of both ordinary citizens and those who had served in the Israeli armed forces. The general sentiment was one of fear and a strong desire for retribution against Hamas.

The global response to the events of October 7, 2023 beween Israel and Palestine has been marked by a call for an immediate ceasefire in Gaza, in acknowledgement of the deepening humanitarian crisis in the region. The United Nations, along with world leaders including President Biden, have expressed grave concerns over the ongoing conflict. Biden and others warned that Israel was starting to lose international support and emphasized the need for the creation of an independent Palestinian state. This stance indicates a shift in the traditional diplomatic positioning of some countries toward the conflict.

These geopolitical developments drive home the point of how interconnected our global community is. The ripple effect of these events has profoundly impacted companies far and wide, not just in the immediate region.

In my role as an advisor to many large corporations, I've seen firsthand the challenges leaders face in managing diverse teams, particularly where people have strong beliefs and points of view, as Israeli and Palestinian employees, suppliers, partners, and customers naturally do about the current situation. These tensions demand that decision-makers employ both empathy and understanding in defining their mission, communicating its parameters, and building the team they expect to implement it. It's a stark reminder of how world events can affect our decision-making and operations in real time, even when they happen thousands of miles away.

As for the global response to the events of October 7th, it will involve a complex and continuing interplay of diplomatic statements, calls for de-escalation, and possibly emergency meetings at international organizations like the United Nations. Countries and international bodies typically express concerns over such escalations and urge both parties to return to negotiations or observe ceasefires. The exact nature of the global response will depend on the specifics of the events that take place over subsequent months, and the stances of various countries and international bodies involved in Middle East diplomacy.

The global response underscores the complexity of the conflict and the challenges involved in finding a lasting solution. While there is a broad consensus on the need to address the humanitarian crisis, the underlying political and territorial disputes will continue to fuel tensions.

For decision-makers, developments like those in Israel and Palestine add further complexity to an already turbulent marketplace. Suppliers, employees, and customers are all affected, and whether places of business or families are being impacted directly, there is no doubt that world events help shape the context in which leaders must make decisions.

Ongoing tensions between Israel and Palestine, Russia's invasion of Ukraine, the pandemic, election upsets throughout the world, etc., inevitably have far-reaching effects. This is why I'm often called in to work with corporations and with governments to help them achieve the best possible outcomes during volatile times. I fully recognize that my experiences mean that I think a little differently, which often helps me offer a fresh perspective and advice that is tangible and practical.

Mission Command: Looking to the Military

Drawing inspiration from the military, the importance of defining a mission cannot be overstated. The military's process includes gathering vital information and then establishing a mission grounded in clear priorities. Once this mission is solidified, it is articulated in a manner that includes clearly outlined objectives, ensuring that everyone involved understands its significance.

Defining the mission is harder than it sounds. It would not work very well if generals simply told the army that their mission was to go off and "win the war." No one would have known, specifically, what they were trying to accomplish or why.

Nor is it particularly helpful when a company simply defines their mission as "to make as much money as possible" or to "sell X% more than last year." These are not well-crafted missions that people can get behind or see as having a true purpose. Which is why they fail.

Experience has shown us again and again that when navigating tasks and responsibilities, lists can be powerful allies. They are simple to make and there are lots of "apps" to help. However, every day I see organizations struggle with the simple concept of defining tasks, assigning responsibility, providing the necessary authority to get things done, and then giving people the space to work through problems.

Lists are essential tools that help us categorize tasks, decide on priorities, and monitor our progress. The structure provided by lists offers a clear plan to follow and gives a tangible record of accomplishments. To put it simply, they help get stuff done.

It's also crucial that everyone understand the parameters of the mission. It's not just about knowing what the mission entails, but also understanding what isn't involved in the mission. This clarity is achieved by defining which activities are acceptable and which aren't. It further involves setting specific timelines, deciding on the dynamics of collaboration, and pinpointing the expected outcomes.

Such a comprehensive approach ultimately ensures that a strategic and systematic method will be adopted to tackle challenges and seize opportunities. Empathy will be preserved, the unique characteristics of the moment will be considered, and elements that promote optimization of the mission will be recognized and included in the planning.

The art of intelligence gathering is pivotal in any decision-making process. This involves collecting diverse data points while emphasizing the importance of objectivity. It's not just about the quantity of data, but also about its quality, which is best ensured through triangulation and sourcing from multiple avenues. It's essential to collect this data using varied methods over acceptable time frames, to maintain a clear perspective and prevent biases from creeping in.

Objective analysis demands that data points be scrutinized within the moment's context and the mission's defined parameters. By adhering to fundamental principles and employing simple methods, we can discern patterns. At times, diving deeper into the analysis with further questions can provide invaluable insights.

A team's composition will play a fundamental role in a mission's success. A cohesive team, even if made up of individuals unfamiliar with each other initially, can make all the difference. People are naturally drawn to teams that have a defined purpose, offer a supportive environment, value shared beliefs, provide learning opportunities and acknowledge individual contributions.

It's of utmost importance to communicate the mission to the team in a lucid manner. Addressing the how, why, when and for whom ensures everyone will be on the same page.

When it comes to implementation, roles and responsibilities should be delineated clearly. Leaders shouldn't just command, but share power and earn trust. The focus should be on fostering loyalty, teamwork, and cooperation.

For campaigns, it's essential to maintain a consistent message and theme. While the tactics might need some adaptation, they should always align with and support the mission's broader objectives. And as one mission concludes, it's time to look to the next. This will perpetuate the cycle of success.

By diligently adhering to these principles and methods, organizations can make informed decisions, operate as a united front, and efficiently respond during critical moments.

Navigating Global Shifts in Supply Chains and Supply Chain Ownership

The advent of globalization has created interdependencies that limit ownership and control over supply chains and production capabilities. Geographical constraints dictate where resources are available, making organizations prisoners of geography.

As an example, consider the microchip supply chain.

Back in the day, businesses knew who they were getting supplies from, who they were up against, and who they were selling to. And these things pretty much stayed the same for decades. In today's interconnected world, however, the dynamics of globalization have redefined supply chain ownership.

Due to these changes, businesses don't always feel they're in control. They're intertwined with countless entities across the globe, a phenomenon very evident when you consider the microchip supply chain.

Years ago, businesses had a stronghold on every aspect of their operations. They knew their inputs, suppliers and the market they operated in like the back of their hand. But now, the terrain is different. With tensions rising and the world undergoing rapid changes, we've seen how easily the supply of microchips can be disrupted, particularly by events unfolding along Asia's coastal regions, specifically those that relate to Taiwan.

The Taiwan example highlights the complexities and vulnerabilities of the global supply chain for microchips, which are crucial components in a wide array of technology. Furthermore, it's an example that reveals how the combination of global interdependence, concentrated production, geopolitical tensions, and rapid technological change can make a particular supply chain vulnerable to disruptions, particularly in politically sensitive areas.

Several key factors are at play when we focus on potential discontinuities in the global microchip supply chain:

- **Global Interdependence:** The production and supply of microchips involve a highly interconnected global network. Key components might be manufactured in one country, assembled in another, and then integrated into final products in yet another. This interdependence means that disruptions in one part of the world can ripple through the entire supply chain.

- **Concentration of Production:** Much of the world's microchip production is concentrated in a few geographic areas, particularly in East Asia. Countries like China, Taiwan (home to TSMC, one of the world's largest semiconductor manufacturers), South Korea and Japan play pivotal roles in the microchip supply chain.

- **Geopolitical Tensions:** Rising geopolitical tensions, especially involving major chip-producing regions, can severely impact the supply chain. For example, tensions between China and other countries could lead to trade restrictions or sanctions, disrupting the flow of materials and finished products. The situation could be exacerbated by territorial disputes or military activities in sensitive regions, such as the South China Sea, which is the nexus of a vital shipping route.

- **Rapid Technological Change:** The demand for microchips is constantly evolving due to rapid technological advancements. The need for more sophisticated and powerful chips in sectors like consumer electronics, the automotive industry, and industrial machinery puts additional pressure on the supply chain.

- **Events Along or Near China's Coast:** Specific events, such as military exercises, territorial disputes, or political standoffs in or near Chinese coastal areas could disrupt shipping routes or manufacturing operations. These events could lead to delays, increased costs, and shortages in the global market.

But No Pressure, Right?

The pressures on decision-makers today are enormous. Between the demands of both local and global governments, the magnifying lens of the media, interest groups with their powerful agendas, and the needs of the business community from suppliers to sellers, the impact on decision-making is immense. As if navigating these scenarios isn't frustrating enough, decision-makers also need to factor in the whims of the market, personal family considerations and the ever-present demands of shareholders.

Balancing these myriad concerns is quite the juggling act.

Ethical Considerations

For all businesses, regardless of size, there's always a tussle between doing what's ethical and moral and what might be profitable. Business leaders grapple with where to allocate resources, choosing between reinvesting in the business, contributing to society or enhancing employee welfare.

At the same time, they're constantly walking the tightrope between ensuring product quality and increasing production quantity to drive profits. And then there's the environmental and societal implications of every decision, not to mention the rapidly evolving challenges of our time, which make traditional decision-making techniques seem far less relevant.

The Moment

Pivoting to another crucial idea, there's this thing I like to call "The Moment." Life is full of disruptions, but every so often, there's a seismic shift, or a special opportunity. It could be good or bad: perhaps it is a chance meeting, a car accident, or something someone said to you that stopped you in your tracks. Perhaps a car bomb went off in a crowded market. Maybe it was the birth of your child. Maybe you have the chance to hire someone in your company who will make significant changes. It's these moments that present the most profound challenges, but also the greatest opportunities.

Bringing us back to military training, the ability to swiftly and effectively respond to these seismic shifts, relying on both leadership and teamwork, becomes paramount. What sets successful organizations apart is their knack for not just making it through these moments, but truly making the most of them. In fact, these organizations anticipate them, which is why responses to these shifts were integrated into their plan and didn't derail it.

When I talk about The Moment, I mean game-changing points in time, those instances when the status quo can be overthrown. The real magic lies in recognizing these moments and harnessing their potential. But it's not just about carpe diem (seizing the moment); it's about making informed decisions within The Moment. This means relying on accurate information, sidestepping potential pitfalls from misleading data, and setting a clear, progressive agenda for the mission.

Expectation management is a huge part of this equation. Organizations need to calibrate their capabilities to line up with what's expected of them, ensuring transparency, integrity, and ethical behavior every step of the way. This is where true leaders shine, by taking responsibility and making every team member feel valued. If there's dysfunction within a team, it's often a symptom of leadership dropping the ball.

But how do we define success in these transformative moments? It's not as simple as looking at numbers or metrics. It's an experience, or a feeling, if you will. Core values are the compass here, guiding decisions and ensuring that plans align with what an organization truly represents. In essence, achieving goals that resonate with these core values and beliefs is the real measure of success. Using this as a foundation, organizations are better equipped to handle the intricacies of our modern world.

In this whirlwind, decision-makers really need to be on their toes, crafting strategies that account for all the shifts, always remaining one step ahead.

Catching that Game-Changing Moment

Life is full of unexpected twists and turns, and sometimes, we experience moments that flip our world upside down. They make us rethink everything we thought we knew.

And you know what? Over time, we get better at dealing with these curve balls. It's like that military training I talked about earlier - we learn to respond in the nick of time, building leadership skills and camaraderie. The real winners are the organizations that spot these moments and totally rock them.

These are the game-changers - the times when everything can shift, breaking our usual rhythm. The trick is spotting them and using them to our advantage.

Making choices during these times is critical. We need the real deal - accurate info - to make the best calls. Dodging mistakes because of bad data is key. Regardless of how we conceptualize the mission, it should be all about moving forward, not just going back to the old ways.

Managing the Hype

Expectations can make or break you. Companies need to be abundantly clear about what they can do and what folks should expect.

Being transparent, honest, and ethical, especially during tough times, is a must. And leaders? They've got to step up, own their roles and make everyone feel they're part of something bigger. When a team falls apart it's often because the leader didn't step up.

What's the Score?

Defining what "winning" looks like during these moments can be a brain teaser. It's more about how people feel than about some numbers on a chart. Our values should light the way, guiding us as we make tough calls. All plans should jibe with these values, addressing the big questions like what we're gunning for, how soon we want it and why. At the end of the day, nailing it in these moments means hitting targets that sync up with our beliefs and our core. By really getting The Moment and making value-driven choices, organizations are perfectly set up to tackle today's wild world.

The Importance of Empathy

In every situation we face, whether monumental or minute, people are always at the heart of the matter. It's essential to remember this, especially when making important decisions. At the core of it all, empathy should be our compass, guiding every choice we make.

Optimizing these crucial moments in life demands a deep understanding of our priorities. It might seem like a no-brainer, but when we're caught up in the thick of things, it's this crystal-clear clarity that helps us filter out the noise and distractions, allowing us to zero in on what's genuinely important: the people around us.

But understanding doesn't stop there. To truly make effective decisions, we need to listen actively, genuinely hearing what others have to say and striving to see the world through their eyes. It's this kind of empathy that illuminates what matters most and shapes our decisions accordingly.

What drives our decisions? A genuine compassion for humanity should be at the helm. When our choices are aligned with our values, decision-making becomes almost intuitive, requiring less thinking. Recognizing the untapped potential in people, and seeing beyond their apparent limits, is a skill in itself.

When we collaborate with these individuals to dig deep within to unearth their strengths, often nudging them into challenging scenarios and then being their pillar of support during tough times, it's not just a job well done; it's our duty.

Speaking of duty, in today's world, teeming with strife and unease, having a steadfast sense of duty makes all the difference. This commitment to always do the right thing, this ethical grounding, it's what sets truly remarkable individuals and organizations apart. It's crucial, then, for both individuals and organizations to wear their beliefs and values on their sleeves, letting these principles guide them like the North Star through the complex maze of decision-making.

Empathy and Listening

Yet, before we set out to make a positive impact on others, there's a prerequisite that must be met, and it is this: we must have confidence. We need to have faith in our own abilities. Through my experience I've discovered this type of confidence can blossom through teamwork and trust, nurtured over time by shared experiences.

The tales we hear from conflict zones might seem worlds apart from our daily reality. But they underscore the timeless importance of clarity, empathy and listening. By taking a moment to slow down, to consider diverse viewpoints during these times, we begin to see the thread of shared humanity that runs through all of us, binding us together regardless of the conflicts or crises that may loom large.

Optimizing the Moment is a multifaceted endeavor. First of all, understanding our priorities is paramount. While this might sound straightforward, when we are caught up in the heat of the moment our priorities must remain crystal clear and not become clouded by emotion. Discovering our true priorities alleviates the burden of unnecessary worry. Often, when we undergo transformative experiences or face pivotal moments, our perspectives shift, leading us to disregard trivial concerns. Through this understanding we gain unparalleled clarity and focus, and this helps us learn to cherish the people around us.

Optimize the Moment

It is essential to truly see and hear the people who surround us, who form our networks of supporters and co-workers. Actively listening to their perspectives enriches our worldview. I recognize this runs counter to the way we've all been taught to handle business, but this cultivated empathy allows us to truly appreciate what's vital in life. Effective decision making necessitates this appreciation, as if it forces us to acknowledge the broader context of the world.

Delving into our motivations, we find that compassion for humanity can significantly influence our decisions, aligning them with what truly matters. Decision-making rooted in core values is often more straightforward; when our decisions resonate with our values, we don't have to dwell on them too long. This can help defuse interpersonal conflicts, such as those we have with people at work or those that emerge during the dreaded social media discourse that too often sucks us in.

Another critical aspect is learning to understand people, discerning the nuances of situations, and recognizing potential opportunities. We must acknowledge the innate capacities all people possess – often, they're capable of much more than they or we believe. It's our duty to help individuals recognize their strengths and worthiness. This often involves placing them in challenging scenarios where failure is a possibility. But it's through these trials, and with the subsequent support we offer, that they can truly come into their own.

There's a profound sense of fulfillment in doing good for others. By harnessing our abilities to make a positive impact, we not only celebrate small victories but also recognize their larger implications. Acts of kindness often have a ripple effect, encouraging others to pay it forward.

In the backdrop of a world teeming with conflict, anxiety, and angst, adhering to a sense of honor becomes a significant differentiator, both for individuals and more pronouncedly in organizations. This sense of honor is intertwined with a sense of duty, underpinned by ethical responsibility. The ethics that guide our actions, behaviors, and methods of governance, especially in pressing moments, are typically reflections of our personal moral codes.

Our beliefs, whether anchored in faith or personal convictions, form the bedrock of our convictions and actions. For organizations, it's beneficial to articulate these beliefs, make them public, and even prominently display them to foster a cohesive culture. Values, those fundamental truths we hold as morally correct, should steer our decisions.

And to be in the best position to assist others, we must have confidence in our abilities. Building this confidence often involves collaboration, embracing our vulnerability, and a series of small, trust-building steps, culminating in unwavering mutual respect and a determination to look out for each other's interests.

Drawing parallels with real-world scenarios, stories from conflict zones starkly contrast with our daily experiences, emphasizing as they do the importance of clarity. These stories underscore the need to genuinely see and hear people, to slow down and fully inhabit the moment. They urge us to consider various facets of a situation, recognizing the universality of such moments across different contexts.

The importance of the act of deciding, especially in business, cannot be overstated. Decisions set the direction, and their absence can be detrimental. The consequences of decisions, particularly their impact on people, magnifies their significance. Making good decisions in the heat of the moment becomes a testament to one's character and judgment.

Moments, after all, represent forks in the road in our lives. While some choose to be mere spectators, others take the lead, and thrive when doing so.

Decision-Making in the Moment

Decisions hold paramount importance in business because they not only provide direction, but also have a profound impact on people's lives.

Surprisingly, the inability to make decisions can be just as consequential, if not more so. Drawing parallels from the theater of war, soldiers often find themselves in perilous situations, where their very survival hinges on making snap decisions.

They rely on their extensive training and instinct, without any room for hesitation, emotional reflection, or fear. Their choices stem from their training, previous deliberations and the sense of clarity that comes with a well-planned mission. This is reminiscent of today's volatile business landscape, where change and crises are the norm. Such an environment necessitates quick, objective responses, akin to those made by soldiers involved in war.

One cannot overemphasize the need for clarity in decision-making. Having a clear vision of what you want is only half the battle; articulating it effectively is just as crucial. Reaching this clarity often involves posing challenging questions to oneself, the organization at large and the market, and then having the audacity to pursue the answers without concern for what you might discover.

But every decision, regardless of its size or significance, carries with it consequences. It's essential to measure and contemplate these outcomes, acknowledging that our choices don't exist in isolation but instead send ripples throughout our interconnected world.

The global arena presents its own set of challenges. Geopolitical upheavals, such as Russia's incursion into Ukraine, China's burgeoning global influence, Iran's nuclear pursuits, and the ensuing global divisions, weigh heavily on business relations and decision-making processes.

I was recently interviewed for an article for Authority Magazine[5] about Optimizing the Moment. The conversation turned to Russia and Ukraine, and I was asked about globalization.

When I think about globalization, it reminds me of how interdependence can both empower and constrain us. Think of it like this: we've always been prisoners of geography, bound by the natural resources at our doorstep. But with globalization, it's as if the world has become one big neighborhood. Once upon a time, a business had its regular suppliers and its known competitors, and a marketplace where everything was familiar. But now everything has changed, and the bakery we use (or the microchip supplier we rely on) could be thousands of miles away rather than right down the street.

Take Russia's invasion of Ukraine. Many saw it coming, but the world's reaction to it has been monumental. Many companies have faced intense scrutiny for "doing business" with Russia since the invasion. They are perceived to be supporting a regime that is committing war crimes against the Ukrainian people. For many companies this is a moral dilemma, a logistical nightmare, a branding challenge, and a human resources issue like no other.

Needless to say, most business leaders were not prepared for this.

And what about ordinary people?

Sadly, they're caught in the crossfire. It's not just about geopolitics; it's about human stories and interconnected lives disrupted by global decisions.

In essence, what we're seeing is the evolution of leadership, displayed in real time. A shift from a business-as-usual model to a world where ethics, values and global dynamics play a pivotal role. Leadership today

5   Rust, Martin. "Martin Rust on 5 Tips for Accelerating Product Ideation & Innovation." Authority Magazine, Medium, October 31, 2023. https://medium.com/authority-magazine/martin-rust-on-5-tips-for-accelerating-product-ideation-innovation-8d05f3ee6ca6.

Optimize the Moment

isn't just about turning a profit. It also means navigating these complex waters with empathy, foresight and integrity ... the latter being the most important and the most difficult value to preserve.

Walking the Talk

Companies making clear statements publicly, and then following through on them, are exactly what needs to happen to send the right message. Not just internally to their employees but externally to their stakeholders, customers, and the general public. This reinforces the idea that ethical behavior isn't just a token phrase in a mission statement, but an actionable and non-negotiable standard.

It's also essential to have leaders who not only champion values but demonstrate them in their actions. Leadership's behavior becomes a model for the entire organization. If they compromise on ethics, it's much harder to expect the rest of the company to hold itself to a higher standard.

Transparency builds trust. If a company is clear about its values from the start, stakeholders know what to expect. But just saying it isn't enough. They need to walk the talk, consistently.

In this age of social media and rapid information dissemination, it's not just about whether you'll get caught doing something wrong. It's also about building a reputation for doing the right things, in every circumstance. Companies that are proactive in their ethical approach don't just avoid scandals, they earn respect and loyalty.

For consultants and professionals, I think there's a two-fold responsibility. First, to assess whether you can align with a company's values and ethics before engaging with them. And second, if you're already engaged and notice discrepancies in ethical behavior, you should raise concerns and recommend corrective actions. This will help the business and put it on the right side of history, by ensuring that we're contributing to a better corporate culture and, by extension, a better world.

We must be resolute in continuing to enforce and promote that kind of behavior and setting a high level of expectations. It creates a healthy precedent, where everyone is held to the same ethical standards regardless of their position or the revenue they brought in. That singular act can resonate deeply and create ripples across the entire industry.

And acting in this way is more relevant than ever today. In an age where consumers are more educated, more informed, and more discerning about the choices they make, ethical conduct isn't just a luxury or an afterthought – it's a necessity. A company's ethical stance and actions (or inactions) can significantly impact its brand reputation, employee morale and the bottom line. Companies are increasingly being held accountable for their actions, both good and bad, in the court of public opinion.

Companies that prioritize ethical behavior and cultivate an organizational culture that rewards integrity over short-term gains find themselves in a stronger position in the long run. Not only do they attract like-minded talent who are driven by purpose and principles, but they also connect with a clientele that values and supports businesses that stand for something greater than just profit.

Transparency and authenticity have become buzzwords, but it's the actions behind those words that matter. It's not just about saying you're committed to ethics; it's about demonstrating that commitment in every decision and every action, every day.

For those of us who were there, witnessing the actions of companies like Merrill Lynch (which I explain in more detail in a few paragraphs) serves as a reminder that while the path of integrity might be challenging at times, it's always worth it. In the end, the companies that thrive are the ones that recognize that their most valuable asset isn't their product or service, but their reputation—and a reputation built on integrity is the most resilient and enduring of all.

Listening is such a basic, fundamental human need, and yet it's astounding how many organizations and individuals overlook it. When a company or a consultant genuinely listens, they're not just hearing the words, they're understanding the pain points, the desires, and the underlying needs. It's a simple yet powerful approach.

And that's where genuine consulting comes into play. Consulting shouldn't mean imposing a solution. It should be about co-creating a solution based on the unique requirements of the client. It's about understanding the nuances of their business and offering tailored recommendations, rather than a one-size-fits-all strategy. It's about building relationships, earning trust, and delivering value.

There's an old saying that's appropriate here: "If the only tool you have is a hammer, every problem looks like a nail." Many organizations fall into the trap of offering the same solutions to different problems, simply because that's what they're accustomed to doing. But in a rapidly changing world, flexibility, adaptability, and a willingness to react to new circumstances are paramount.

That's why the Deloitte model (which I explain in greater detail further into the book) has been so successful. They understand that each client is unique, each problem distinct, and that solutions should be crafted with care and precision, rather than being churned out from a template. By adopting an entrepreneurial approach and allowing their consultants the freedom to innovate and adapt, they're not just providing a service, they're forging authentic partnerships.

When we strip away all the jargon and complexities, at its core a business is built on human connections. And those connections are best forged through genuine listening and understanding.

So, whether it's a small farm, a multinational corporation, or a government entity, the principle remains the same: listen, understand, and then act. It's a timeless formula and one that will always yield the best results.

Taking a Page from the Merrill Lynch Playbook

I often come back to Merrill Lynch because I felt then and still feel their model was exemplary.

From 1993 until November 2001, I worked at Merrill Lynch Canada, following their acquisition of Midland Walwyn. My roles included Investment Advisor, Branch Manager, and Regional Sales Manager for Southwestern Ontario.

During my tenure, I focused on managing and developing an investment practice dedicated to high-net-worth clients. I was responsible for product development and distribution in one of Canada's largest and most profitable regions, handling $4.5 billion in client assets.

My role involved forming strategic alliances to offer sophisticated investment solutions for individual clients and foundations. This required me to understand complex regulatory issues, compliance policies and system capabilities, as well as trading and reporting issues. I also focused on performance monitoring and relationship management.

During my time at Merrill Lynch, I was part of the International Managers Program, managing a team of senior producers and support staff totaling 250 people. I refer to their incredible business model often because it underscores the age-old debate between long-term vision and short-term gains.

Many companies grapple with the challenge of striking a balance between immediate profitability and sustainability. Cutting costs might offer a quick boost to the bottom line, but at what long-term price?

Merrill Lynch's approach was a lesson in prioritizing core performance, while also factoring in the nuances of customer experience. They acknowledged that while the bells and whistles of enhanced customer service are crucial, they don't mean anything if the fundamental promise isn't kept.

In financial services, that fundamental promise is robust financial performance. It's an approach that focuses on delivering core value first, and then accentuating it with impressive service features.

When I worked for Merrill Lynch, every employee was gifted a plaque that summarized the company's principles. And while it was just a few words, the company's senior leadership put a lot of thought into getting those words just right.

The plaque read the following:

"Respect for the Individual, Teamwork, Integrity,

Client Focus, Responsible Citizenship."

These principles were the bedrock of the organization's culture, reflecting thoughtful deliberation among senior leadership.

And By Contrast...

Today's corporate landscape is riddled with companies making hasty decisions to appear attractive in quarterly reports, often to the detriment of long-term stability and growth. A company shedding its entire administrative layer to boost profitability is a prime example of this phenomenon.

Such decisions might look good in the immediate term, but the long-term effects of such a choice can be detrimental. Administrative functions, often seen as secondary, play a vital role in the smooth functioning of an organization. They are the glue that holds various departments together, ensuring seamless operations and enabling core teams to focus on what they do best.

When an organization makes such a significant change without considering its long-term implications, it's not just changing its structure; it's altering its very DNA. Teams that were used to certain protocols and supports will now need to adapt to an entirely new way of working, which can affect morale, efficiency and, eventually, the quality of output.

This situation brings us back to the principle of understanding the balance between short-term gains and overall value. Companies must always ask themselves: "Are we enhancing or detracting from our core promise?" Cost-cutting measures, reorganizations, or any other strategic decision should always enhance the core promise, not detract from it.

The emphasis on short-term thinking is a concerning trend, especially when it sacrifices an organization's long-term vision and potential. Decision-makers need to look beyond immediate gains and understand the broader implications of their choices. They must recognize the interplay between the immediate and the eventual, between the core promise and the added enhancements. Companies that manage to strike this balance are the ones that not only survive but thrive, especially in the face of turbulent times.

Then there are environmental crises. Disasters like forest fires, hurricanes, rising sea levels and power grid failures are more frequent now than ever. This compels companies to be introspective about the environmental footprints of their operations, which can span everything from mundane office supply choices to intricate production mechanisms. In such a mercurial world, those at the helm must be equipped to make agile yet informed decisions, bearing in mind the ripple effects they might trigger, impacting people, organizations, and our delicate environment.

On an organizational front, challenges come in various forms. There's the daunting task of warding off cyber threats and potential data breaches, efficiently managing technology tools and facilities, and bridging gaps in training, leadership, experience, skills, talent, and knowledge. Ensuring a nurturing organizational culture remains paramount, as does devising strategies to cope with the exit of integral team members. Businesses must also be agile enough to alter their strategies as necessary to stay updated, ensuring they don't fall into the trap of obsolescence.

Personal challenges are equally diverse. They can range from grappling with physical changes or injuries that push us into introspection, to battling dwindling confidence, to traversing traumatic experiences, to reevaluating deeply held beliefs or ideals.

These defining moments call for clarity, comprehension, and decisive action. How we handle these moments profoundly shapes our identity, whether as individuals, organizations, or as part of a broader society. Making decisions during these pivotal times should be a conscious effort and not left to fate.

The very act of deciding is foundational. Everything that follows is essentially logistical.

Optimize the Moment Isn't a Buzzword; It's a Movement Toward Something Sustainable

But what do we mean when we say "Optimize?" When global events constantly impact how governments and businesses function, and when we frequently encounter game-changing moments or crises, how can we make the most of these situations?

This question forms the essence of this book, as we delve deeply into the art of refining our decisions and actions when reaching these crucial crossroads.

Optimizing transcends mere survival or maintaining the status quo. It embodies the idea of constantly striving to do better, not just for ourselves but for our stakeholders, shareholders and employees, and everyone who looks up to us for direction and leadership. This includes our families.

Optimizing doesn't stop at just ensuring survival through adversity. It pushes us to extract the maximum potential from every crisis, situation, opportunity, or resource we come across. Achieving true optimization, however, demands a specific set of skills, consistent practice, unwavering determination, and a purposeful approach.

When we talk about what we desire, it's essential to differentiate between merely winning and achieving. While winning may indicate a terminal success point, continuous achievement implies a persistent pursuit of excellence. This mindset values consistent progress, recognizing success as the process of realizing desired outcomes through concerted effort, skill and/or courage.

Similarly, there's a nuanced difference between objectives and goals. Objectives serve as specific, tangible milestones that guide us to our ultimate goals, which offer a broader vision or purpose. In the decision-making realm, pinpointing and articulating these objectives becomes a crucial task. Moreover, it's vital not to settle for merely "good enough" when there's room for improvement. The essence of optimization is to always be in a state of betterment, ensuring that we're better tomorrow than we are today.

Visualization plays a fundamental role, especially when determining the best possible course of action in any given situation. It's crucial to recognize that the "best" doesn't always equate to reverting to a familiar state or the status quo. Instead, it involves discerning and defining the optimal outcome for that particular moment. Yet, achieving clarity in these critical moments can represent a daunting challenge, given the barrage of information, heightened emotions, and the chaotic nature of crises.

Soldiers on the battlefield, for instance, cultivate a sense of clarity by rigorously training and adopting a structured approach, enabling them to make decisions even under intense pressure. Organizations, too, can attain this level of clarity and direction, arming them with the capability to optimize any situation they confront.

With respect to decisions and actions, optimizing the moment goes beyond just getting by. It involves a commitment to secure the best conceivable outcomes for all stakeholders involved.

It has become increasingly clear that the ability to optimize decisions and actions in pivotal moments is what separates the exceptional from the ordinary. This commitment to securing the best conceivable outcomes for all stakeholders involved is not just about survival; it's about thriving in the face of adversity and uncertainty.

Reflecting on my own journey, I can see how these principles have been a constant guide throughout my career. My time at Merrill Lynch was a period where I learned a lot about interpreting and understanding people, psychology, and deeper motivations. This experience taught me how to listen and to empathize, and to forge a path that aligned with both my clients' aspirations and the wider market dynamics.

September 11, 2001: A Watershed Moment

I look back on those years at Merrill Lynch as some of the most formative of my career. They shaped my understanding of strategic decision making, of balancing individual needs with complex market data and trends and of the importance of clarity and foresight in leadership. Had it not been for the dramatic shift in the world's landscape following the tragic events of September 11, 2001, I might still be there, continuing on that path.

However, life, much like business, is unpredictable. The aftermath of 9/11 was a "moment," a turning point for me, and for much of the world. The geopolitical focus shifted dramatically, and so did my career trajectory. It was a time that called for applying my skills beyond finance and into negotiations, bridge-building, capacity-building, and governance.

The decision by Merrill Lynch to sell off their international business units and focus on U.S. domestic business post-9/11 marked a significant change. It signaled a shift in the company's direction and, for me, a transition to a new phase in my professional life at CIBC Wood Gundy in Canada. This period was a testament to the need for adaptability and resilience – qualities that are essential in optimizing the moment, no matter the circumstances.

These experiences fundamentally shaped my approach to decision-making, strategizing, and navigating the complex tapestry of global business and politics.

How I Came to Optimize the Moment

The Merrill Lynch Days

I started my career working for Midland Walwyn, which became Merrill Lynch in the financial services sector. My job required multiple skills, many of which revolved around listening to people.

Much of the training focused on human psychology and what motivated people through the different phases of their lives. The world of global financial markets is vast and complicated, full of tools and levers that can be employed to help people achieve their goals. Understanding them, and how to employ them properly and at the right time, took training, skill, judgment, and an approach to decision making that was beginning to resonate with me more deeply.

After 9/11, everyone in the world was focused on what was happening geopolitically. In this turbulent climate a "moment" presented itself, and I jumped at the opportunity it provided.

In the wake of 9/11, Merrill Lynch suddenly decided to sell off their international business units, focusing solely on U.S. domestic business. By November, I found myself working for CIBC Wood Gundy in Canada. Even though our clients and services remained largely unchanged, everything was in transition.

The Transition Period

Merrill Lynch had given me exposure to the international marketplace and a taste for engaging in the broader issues that impacted geopolitical events. I wanted to draw upon the experience I had gained to date and do something that would have an impact, somewhere, somehow.

The leadership and strategic planning abilities I developed in wealth management proved to be beneficial. They enabled me to approach issues from a unique perspective, one that combined a deep understanding of economic systems with a practical approach to problem-solving.

The transition from the world of wealth management to overseas development work would for me be both a natural progression and a deliberate choice. I saw it as an opportunity to apply the insights and skills I had gained in the corporate sector to address a variety of challenges.

During the transition, I served as Vice President and Investment Advisor at Lighthouse Private Client Corporation, still working with high-net-worth individuals. It was another "moment" where we took the opportunity to create a sophisticated platform that integrated world-class institutional money managers, which offered our clients exclusive, segregated money management opportunities.

I interacted with both the financial markets and the back office of the firm. I enjoyed the clients, my partners, and the experience immensely. But I knew it wasn't exactly where I needed to be.

It wasn't long before the "moment" presented me with an opportunity to go overseas, to Jakarta, Indonesia, where I would have the chance to apply my skills and sink my teeth into the geopolitical realities of Southeast Asia.

My main focus was negotiations, bridge building, and learning the intricacies of the largest Muslim country on earth. I was there as CEO of WealthFunds SPC, a growing financial services firm involved in product development support and a crucial phase of an international business launch.

This was a fascinating time to be in Indonesia. Located in the heart of Southeast Asia, in the days following 9/11 it was a hub of people from all over the world, many of whom were focused on security concerns and the tensions that arose following the Bali bombings.

The Bali, Indonesia Bombings of 2002

The Bali bombings occurred on October 12, 2002. Paddy's Pub in Kuta Beach was bustling with activity, when at 11:05 p.m. a man detonated a bomb he was carrying in his backpack. Within moments, patrons, both injured and unharmed, poured into the streets, only to be met with an even more massive explosion from a car bomb planted outside the Sari Club, which sat right across from Paddy's.

The timing couldn't have been worse. Kuta Beach was filled with tourists, including several Australian sports teams, there for their annual end-of-season holiday. The devastation caused by the explosion was unprecedented. Buildings neighboring the blast were decimated, and windows shattered blocks away. The explosion was so fierce it left a deep crater in its wake.

The local hospital, Sanglah, was swamped and ill-prepared for an emergency of this magnitude. Burn victims were being submerged in nearby hotel pools to soothe their wounds, simply because the hospital couldn't cope. Many had to be transported vast distances to Darwin and Perth, to receive the care they needed.

There was another smaller blast near the U.S. consulate in Denpasar, which seemed to be a precursor to the Kuta bombings.

In total 202 souls were lost, with the majority being Western tourists and holiday revelers. But among these there were also many local Balinese, people who worked nearby, lived in the vicinity, or were just at the wrong place at the wrong time. Many of those lost were young, in their 20s and 30s. The international community was shaken, and the UN condemned the attack as a threat to global peace.

In the Face of Extreme Adversity, Leaders Emerge

This tragedy was another "moment," for Indonesia, but with broader geopolitical implications. After seizing the opportunity to go to Indonesia, for me these events provided the chance to learn and to understand more about the complexities of the situation.

Human resilience is amazing. I certainly witnessed people with very little who stepped up and led others with purpose, almost in defiance of the challenges they faced.

Coming from Canada and stepping into Indonesia, the cultural disparities between Western and Southeastern Asia were stark and often overwhelming. To be frank, those early days were filled with challenges. Finding purpose, understanding my role, and genuinely making an impact felt impossible.

In thinking about my time and experiences in Southeast Asia now, I can say without reservation that the region truly captivated me. While it is interconnected in many ways, and geographically quite close, each part is distinct. Jakarta is completely different from Kuala Lumpur, which could not be more different than Singapore, each possessing its own historical, cultural and geographical nuances. And yet there is a tapestry of the region that is beautiful, rich, diverse, interwoven. It is also a political and power-seeking minefield.

For me, those days were critical for developing discipline. Having a sound approach was one thing, putting it into practice was another.

Southeast Asia is often described by Westerners as "chaotic" because of the sheer volume of people and traffic, and that would be an accurate description. The pace of business, politics and power transactions are also often chaotic, and played like a game where the rules change after every move.

Discipline. Mission. Parameters of the mission. What are the levers that can be pulled, and which ones can't? Identifying the team. Intelligence gathering. More discipline. These were the drumbeats of those transitional days in Southeast Asia.

It is always important to learn about the environment, and what motivates people to make the decisions they do. Intelligence gathering is about obtaining a variety of data points, collected objectively, without making judgments at the time about their relevance or a potential conclusion.

For example: did you know that Jakarta is sinking, quite literally? This phenomenon is a result of several factors.

One of the primary reasons Jakarta is sinking is excessive extraction of groundwater. Many residents and businesses in Jakarta rely on groundwater, due to inadequate public water supply systems. This excessive pumping of groundwater causes the ground to compact and sink, a process known as subsidence.

Jakarta has also experienced rapid urban development and population growth. This has led to increased construction and the dramatic expansion of the city's building mass, further contributing to its sinking.

Compounding the issue of land subsidence is the global problem of rising sea levels due to climate change. As sea levels rise, the coastal areas of Jakarta are increasingly prone to flooding.

Jakarta's infrastructure, particularly its drainage systems, is not adequately equipped to handle the combination of heavy rainfall, rising sea levels and land subsidence. This has led to frequent and increasingly severe flooding in many parts of the city.

As a result of these factors, some areas of Jakarta are sinking at an alarming rate. And until you've witnessed the rainy season's effects firsthand in places like Bandung and the outskirts of Jakarta, it's hard to grasp the profound nature of the environmental changes occurring there.

Not to mention, Indonesia is situated on the Pacific Ring of Fire, which is subject to frequent earthquakes. The apartment I rented was designed to sway up to 12 feet to accommodate this. Riding horses, which is my favorite hobby, in an area recognized for frequent thunder and lightning storms, felt surreal.

As a consequence of all this, the volume of environmental data points that drive decisions for most companies, or even governments, pale in comparison to those that must be evaluated by decision-makers in Jakarta. Here, simple things like staff being able to get to work during regular flooding is a major concern. Add to that the inconsistent reliability of electric power, the questionable sustainability of computer servers and internet connections, and the constant need for viable communications equipment, and a lot of organizations simply can't function.

Conducting business in Indonesia was an eye-opening experience. Their notion of corruption differed. Whether it was a simple act of mailing a postcard, parking a car, or making it through my interactions with law enforcement, "payoffs" at various levels were routine. It is a societal norm not exclusive to Indonesia, but prevalent in many developing nations.

Transitioning from a technical role in the financial sector to immersing myself in a new culture helped me develop invaluable skills. Listening to and understanding people from diverse backgrounds readied me for my next "moment" in Ukraine, where these competencies proved crucial.

Reflecting on it now, I can humbly admit that those initial phases were tough. My naivety and struggles were perhaps evident to others, even if I was reluctant to acknowledge them myself. But in retrospect, that journey, filled with its many bumps and curves, helped me develop the Optimize the Moment approach.

The National Democratic Institute for International Affairs

During my time in Indonesia, I was very fortunate to be approached by representatives of the National Democratic Institute (NDI) about the possibilities of me working in Ukraine. The NDI is an NGO funded by the U.S. State Department, for the purposes of engaging in capacity-building and governance overseas.

I should offer a few words about this remarkable organization. After my experiences in financial service, it might seem like joining NDI was a 90-degree turn, and that would be fair. The NDI is a non-profit, non-partisan organization, focusing on strengthening democratic institutions globally through citizen participation, openness, and accountability in government. A far stretch from financial services to be sure, but much of my training and experience proved to be relevant.

The NDI has been involved in promoting citizen engagement in politics, supporting democratic governance, ensuring the integrity of electoral processes, and advocating for gender equality in politics. They are dedicated to supporting and strengthening democratic institutions worldwide, and they work in partnership with similar organizations such as the International Republican Institute (IRI), with whom I have also had the privilege to work. Since its founding in 1983, the NDI has collaborated with local partners in 156 countries.

Accomplishing what I needed to, I was called upon to utilize my services in Ukraine.

The Orange Revolution in Ukraine

Before heading to Ukraine, I felt privileged to meet with former Ambassador Nelson Ledsky in Washington, D.C. Amb. Ledsky was an American diplomat renowned for being Ronald Reagan's National Security Adviser.

Amb. Ledsky was an incredible individual, widely admired. Along with former Secretary of State Madeleine Albright, they saw opportunities for "moments" where private individuals with certain kinds of knowledge could have conversations and accomplish things that traditional diplomats could not. This work was often carried out by non-Americans, in areas like political party development, civil society building and governance.

I had flown from Jakarta to Hong Kong, to Anchorage, to Dulles Airport, to meet with Amb. Ledsky. After the meeting and the briefing it entailed, I flew to Heathrow, then Amsterdam, and eventually, I reached Kyiv. If you trace that journey on a globe, you would see that I covered nearly three-quarters of the circumference of the planet through the air.

Once I arrived at my hotel in Kyiv, I needed to eat and decided to enter the first restaurant I came across. To my surprise, after leaving Indonesia the first place I found only served Asian food. There I was, in the middle of Kyiv, eating with chopsticks. Sometimes we really do arrive where we started.

In Ukraine, it was quickly apparent that my perspective needed adapting. Observing so-called 'ordinary' individuals seizing "moments" and rising against the norm was inspiring - especially for the women of Ukraine. For decades, they had been oppressed and not allowed to have opinions of their own. Yet, in those "moments," here they were taking stands on issues. The Orange Revolution became emblematic of their resilience and determination. Those orange ribbons symbolized their newfound voice. For the first time, they had the liberty to vote, partake in politics, and engage in democracy.

Witnessing this societal transformation was deeply moving. Observing these individuals challenge long-held beliefs and traditions was not only a lesson in courage but also a privilege. The people who supported and facilitated this change each represented a separate thread in the grand tapestry of this transformation.

For those who aren't aware, the Orange Revolution was a surge of civil unrest that roiled Ukraine in the latter part of 2004. At the heart of it was a contentious presidential election between Viktor Yushchenko and Viktor Yanukovych, believed to be tainted by corruption and electoral manipulation.

This belief wasn't unfounded; Kyiv saw an influx of protestors day after day, championing a fair political landscape. When foreign and local entities flagged the election as suspicious, it culminated in a revote, leading to Yushchenko's winning by a significant margin.

However, this wasn't just a simple protest. It was deeply rooted in Ukraine's recent history.

There was the tale of journalist Georgiy Gongadze's unsettling murder, for example, rumored to have been orchestrated by then-President Leonid Kuchma. This incident had already stirred civil discontent, and by the time 2004 arrived many saw it as a backdrop to the current tensions. Adding to this was Ukraine's complicated relationship with its past, particularly its Soviet ties, and a growing sense of national identity distinct from that era.

A key ingredient in the Orange Revolution was the younger generation. These were individuals who had grown disillusioned by the political elite, yearning for a more genuine leadership. They resonated with Yushchenko's transparent demeanor, viewing him as a beacon of hope amidst a backdrop of political scandals and systemic corruption.

The Orange Revolution was not just a political protest. It was an awakening, a sign of renewed vigor for democratic values, and a testament to the spirit of the Ukrainian people.

In Eastern Europe, particularly in the communist era, the government's stranglehold on people's personal freedoms was palpable. It wasn't merely applied to women, but to the entire populace.

Opinions? Those were a luxury. It wasn't so much about what attire you wore, but more about where you went, what you did and when you did it. Living under that system meant conforming to an overarching script laid down by the state. This was an entirely different beast from the oppressions we often associate with religious dogmas, especially what was experienced by women in some regions dominated by patriarchal religious systems.

Optimizing the Moment at Warp Speed

Trust-building involves listening, spending time with people, and engaging. But in Ukraine my time was limited, and when we didn't have the luxury of time we needed to lean on intermediaries. If Ukrainians trusted a local figure and that figure vouched for you, that became your path to building trust. It was an indirect yet efficient strategy given the circumstances.

Adding to the challenges was a lack of knowledge of a difficult language, and again, local colleagues proved to be invaluable. I was privileged to have moments with them and share insights into their lives and their families. It was a real gift to watch and to listen, to see them work at building a better society, not necessarily knowing what that looked like but motivated only by a sense of purpose that brought them together. They were unbelievably passionate.

Ukraine, with its unique historical tapestry and geopolitical intricacies, stands as a testament to humanity's adaptability and resilience. On a wider scale, their story illuminates the personal dimensions of globalization. It moves beyond mere market dynamics and economic systems to emphasize the core human elements: traditions, customs, challenges, and dreams.

Their narratives weave a vibrant depiction of the diverse human experiences, adversities and successes that define our globally connected society. Here, I witnessed the valor of everyday Ukrainians as they championed change, their resilience and willpower incredible. Particularly impressive was the rise in women's empowerment during this era, marking a period where they could outspokenly express their viewpoints for the first time.

Engaging with volunteers or community constituents isn't analogous to navigating traditional work environments. These individuals are driven by fervor, dedication, and an unwavering faith in a cause, rather than mere occupational obligations. Being on the ground, one couldn't help but be moved by their dedication to that cause and newfound beliefs and values. It was hard not to be affected and informed by the experience.

This ethos isn't limited to global endeavors; it's foundational to any human-centric quest. Cultivating trust, valuing everyone's input, and affirming their significance are the linchpins of productive interactions. Regardless of the geographical or cultural backdrop, the innate human desire to belong and to be acknowledged is universal.

In the diverse settings I experienced, including Indonesia and Ukraine, my role was never one defined by authority. Instead, I saw myself as a facilitator, a confidant, and a student. My mission was to learn about their viewpoints, the obstacles they faced, and the cultural intricacies they embraced, integrating them into our broader ambitions.

Between all that I learned and being immersed in the culture and the resilience of the people, I could have stayed in Ukraine. But it was time for me to move on to Jordan.

Jordan's Decade: Navigating Tensions, Refugees and Political Shifts

Jordan presented a unique experience to me, its captivating beauty standing out distinctly. While living there, I became involved with the broader region, frequently traveling to cities like Beirut, Cairo, and all over Jordan—a country I became particularly fond of. I was able to take my children with me to explore some of the many wonders of Jordan.

Canada has a strong connection with Jordan (as does the United States), a sign of our extensive assistance and collaboration in the Middle East. This isn't just about strategic geopolitics; it's a commitment founded on shared principles. Both nations advocate for a sustainable resolution to the ongoing conflicts in Syria, Iraq, and the Israeli-Palestinian territories.

Our mutual aspirations encompass:

- Countering terrorism in all its guises;
- Ensuring protection for refugees;
- Channeling humanitarian aid;
- Boosting trade and exploring commercial ventures;
- Advocating for inclusive education, transparent governance, and steady economic progress;
- And importantly, empowering women in the economic sphere.

The connection between Canadians and Jordanians runs deep. This is evident from the Jordanian-Canadian diaspora, which includes a growing number of Jordanians pursuing education in Canada and Canadians making a life in Jordan. We've solidified our presence in Jordan, specifically through our embassy in Amman, and this presence was heightened during the Syrian crisis. Jordan reciprocates through its embassy located in Ottawa.

In the past five years, via our Middle East engagement strategy, Canada has infused over $575.7 million into the Jordanian economy, bolstering Jordan's stability and countering the ripple effects from unrest in neighboring Iraq and Syria.

The number of Syrian refugees in Jordan is staggering. Official records cite around 669,497, but taking unregistered refugees into account, this figure could climb to as high as 1.3 million. Jordan's compassionate stance is also evident in its hosting of refugees from a plethora of nations, like Iraq, Yemen and, of course, Palestine.

When we talk about trade, it's significant to note that Jordan is Canada's inaugural Arab trading partner via Free Trade Agreement. In 2021 alone, our bilateral trade soared to $180 million in value.

We've diversified our exports to Jordan, spanning:

- The automotive sector, notably used vehicles.
- The FMCG sector, which includes agriculture/food and everyday consumer items.
- Healthcare, with an emphasis on wellness products and medical apparatus.
- The energy sector, focusing on billing interfaces for renewable energy firms and distributors.
- Defense, with exports like helicopters, armored transports, and tactical equipment.

My time in Jordan began in 2006. For some context: prior to that, the security situation was tense, not only because of the war in neighboring Iraq, but because events had spilled over into Jordan. In April 2004, authorities intercepted cars loaded with explosives and detained multiple individuals who were believed to have connections with al-Qaeda. Reportedly, their plan was a chemical bomb attack targeting the intelligence services HQ in Amman.

Then in March 2005, Jordan reinstated its ambassador to Israel. The ambassador had been previously recalled in 2000, responding to the eruption of the Palestinian uprising.

By August of the same year, the country faced another security threat. Al-Qaeda launched three missiles from Jordanian soil. While two of these projectiles narrowly missed US naval ships docked in Aqaba, the third missile hit near Israel's Eilat airport. Tragically, a Jordanian soldier lost his life in this attack.

The situation further intensified in November 2005. Jordan was plunged into mourning as suicide bombers targeted three of Amman's international hotels, leading to the tragic loss of sixty lives. Al-Qaeda in

Iraq claimed responsibility. It is important to note that a majority of the casualties were Jordanian citizens.

The ongoing saga with al-Qaeda in Iraq took a significant turn in June 2006, when Iraq's prime minister made a momentous announcement: the Jordanian-born Abu Musab al-Zarqawi, the notorious leader of al-Qaeda in Iraq, had met his demise in an airstrike.

These were tumultuous times in Jordan, but also times of significant progress. July 2007 marked Jordan's first local elections since the turn of the millennium. However, the elections were marred by controversy. The primary opposition, the Islamist Action Front, withdrew from the race, accusing the government of manipulating the vote.

Later that year, in November, parliamentary elections reinforced the positions of tribal leaders and pro-government figures. The previously influential opposition, the Islamic Action Front, witnessed a decline in their fortunes. This political reconfiguration saw Nader Dahabi, known for his moderate views, take on the role of prime minister.

Strategic Governance and Mission Alignment in Post-War Iraq

It was during my tenure with NDI that I was deployed to Iraq. In Iraq, my mission was clear: to provide specialized analysis and guidance to key political figures striving to establish a stable and inclusive government. This mission aligned perfectly with Merrill Lynch's principles. My primary focus was on collaborating closely with the Committees of the Council of Representatives (COR) to craft achievable objectives and detailed action plans. Working in tandem with Cabinet Ministers and senior government officials, I worked with a remarkable team that contributed, in our own small way, to helping those leaders shape a vision for Iraq's future.

However, my responsibilities extended beyond strategic planning. They encompassed communication and the practical implementation of diverse techniques, skills, and strategies—crucial elements for fostering mutual understanding among disparate groups within Iraq's complex and ever-changing environment.

Governance Vs. Mission

When a country is in conflict, there is a lot of mistrust of systems, i.e. the government. As Governance Director, it was my job to build a team of advisors who worked with elected Parliamentarians and officials so they could make better decisions about rebuilding their country. We were there to advise them and help them get on their feet.

The idea was to restore confidence in the citizens, which by this time had decayed quite badly—and their level of mistrust was understandable, given their nation's recent history. They'd watched their country being torn apart, and now with a newly installed government they were not yet convinced of the good intentions of their new leaders. In this situation, it was normal to have apprehension.

Governance and mission are two fundamental aspects of any organization—be it the government, a nonprofit or a for-profit company—and they play distinct roles in shaping its identity and guiding its actions.

Governance, in essence, is the framework of rules, structures and processes that an organization puts in place to ensure its smooth operation. It encompasses the legal and regulatory aspects that govern an organization's activities. You can think of it as the scaffolding that holds everything together. Governance defines how decisions are made, who has the authority to make those decisions, and how accountability is established. It's about setting up the guardrails to ensure that the organization operates within legal and ethical boundaries.

As for the mission, it is not a mere statement; it's the North Star that inspires and motivates everyone within the organization. It answers the fundamental question: "Why do we exist?" A strong mission provides a sense of direction and a higher calling, uniting individuals in a shared purpose. It's what gets people out of bed in the morning, eager to contribute to something larger than themselves.

In summary, governance is about creating the structure and rules that allow an organization to function efficiently and responsibly, while mission is about defining the heart and purpose that gives life and meaning to the organization's actions. Both are essential, and finding the right balance between them is key to the success and sustainability of any organization.

Iraq presents an interesting case study. It was quite distinct from other conflict zones I'd been in, since it was an active conflict zone at the time of my deployment. The other deployments I was involved in, by definition, fall into the category of post-conflict zones. While they may face ongoing challenges, they are generally considered post-conflict in terms of industry development and business.

Regarding the Middle East crisis, it's grounded in a long-standing set of issues with deep-rooted complexities. The recent escalation between Israel and Palestine was a matter of when, not if, for those who have been closely monitoring the situation. These events have been unfolding in alignment with scenarios that have been foreseen for decades, which is undeniably tragic.

When such conflicts play out, especially on our screens, it serves as a stark reminder of the sacrifices made for democracy and freedom. It's crucial to appreciate the significance of governance, politics, and democratic institutions, which are sometimes taken for granted.

Governance matters and respecting the rule of law is essential. The separation of powers, principles, and values is vital in upholding the institutions that underpin our societies. Events like these underscore the importance of protecting and cherishing the freedoms and democracy we enjoy in the West.

In post-conflict zones, the focus shifts to establishing and consolidating governance. This involves clarifying roles, defining decision-making processes, and promoting respect for the rule of law. These regions need to transition from unstructured environments to ones where governance and effective decision-making become the norm.

In Iraq, for example, the challenge was to advise them in how to craft solid legislation that aligned with the country's constitution and addressed practical issues. Over time, we witnessed positive changes, such as better budget management, infrastructure improvements, and the restoration of essential services. These improvements demonstrated the impact of effective governance on people's lives.

A Little Pre-Saddam History

As we journey across Iraq's history to the modern corporate landscape, we encounter a significant shift in governance in 1968. This is when the Iraqi parliament was established, marking a pivotal moment that separated the legislative and judicial branches. This development laid the groundwork for an extensive body of law that lawmakers could draw upon, which would be fundamental to governance and effective decision-making.

Fast forward to the critical year of 2003, a turning point for Iraq, when the transitional administrative law was adopted following the fall of Saddam Hussein. During Saddam's regime, a Shura Council played a significant role, acting as a religious Supreme Court in Iraq, responsible for interpreting both religious and secular laws. This reflected the country's status as a religious state, where religious law was deeply integrated into the governance system.

Then, in August 2008, King Abdullah of Jordan made a highly symbolic move. He traveled to Iraq, becoming the first Arab leader to do so since the American-led invasion in 2003.

The Evolving Role of Women in Iraqi Society

In the Middle East, as in many cultures worldwide, there's a traditional patriarchal structure where men predominantly hold the decision-making power. Women, especially young women, were often expected to follow their father's directives, including how they should vote. This reflected a long-standing expectation that they shouldn't have independent opinions. This deeply rooted cultural norm dated back hundreds, if not thousands of years.

This observation isn't a criticism, but an acknowledgment of cultural history, which in every part of the world is constantly in evolution (we should remember that women didn't earn the right to vote in either Canada or the United States until 1920).

I remember a time when a particular community in Iraq was at a juncture, grappling with a recurring issue that had persisted for decades. The same group of men was deliberating on their next steps, even seeking my perspective on the matter.

Meanwhile a colleague of mine had been extensively engaging with youth, seeking their insights. From my own conversations with young Iraqi men and women, it became evident that there were exceptionally bright young women involved in various civil society groups that were seeking change.

In academic and think tank circles, the term "civil society groups" is often used. It broadly refers to various factions in society, ranging from political action committees to grassroots organizations, that focus on specific community activities, like organizing games for local children. It covers a vast spectrum of community engagement. Civil society groups can vary in size, from small, specialized collectives to expansive organizations.

In the realm of international development, there are typically three main sectors.

First, there's governance, which encompasses the machinery of the government, its decision-making processes, and its various institutions. Second, there are political parties, with certain groups and individuals in the developing world offering advisory and capacity-building services to nurture these parties at different stages of their evolution.

Finally, there's the vast category of civil society groups. This category has various subgroups within it, such as women's collectives, youth organizations, electoral monitoring entities, and election reform factions. Many of the global election monitoring entities, despite their significant and commendable work, can still be classified as actors in civil society.

From my time in Iraq, I remember one young woman in particular, around 17 years old, who bravely voiced her perspective about her community's challenges, emphasizing the importance of reimagining the future. This young woman spoke up bravely, very aware that she was talking about her future and that of her siblings and peers. Although we provided the platform, it was entirely up to her to leverage it, which she did well. She saw the "moment," and she grasped it.

A few men in the gathering dismissed her thoughts, as could have been predicted. Yet many were swayed, not just by the substance of her message but also by the passion in her voice. It's fair to say that this was a transformative "moment" for them as well as for this remarkable young woman.

Over time, my work led me to Kurdistan, and eventually, I found myself in Baghdad, specifically in the Green Zone.

The time I spent there was eye-opening to me. I met some amazing people, witnessed some incredible acts of courage, and saw unlikely allies grasping the "moments" to try to make their country safe and better. I was truly humbled by their stories, by their sacrifices, and by their immutable sense of mission and purpose.

In some cases, despite losing loved ones, their homes, or even suffering major injuries, they somehow managed to get up in the morning to continue following a path they believed in, often leading others, often not from their tribe or background. I was deeply affected by these experiences and humbled, and they changed my thinking and approach to life completely.

After my time in Iraq ended, I returned to Ottawa to establish a home base and reconnect with my family. I needed some grounding. Fortunately, life is full of "moments," and I was able to continue serving on "technical assignments" in places like Pakistan and Tunisia, where I was again given the opportunity to witness remarkable people doing brave things during those watershed moments. They were pursuing what the late Senator John McCain used to call "a cause greater than self."

The vantage point I gained during these adventures, in my exposures to society-altering events, people, and challenges, has truly informed my thinking and perspective today. These experiences have been a gift, this is undeniable.

Madeleine Albright's Influence

Madeleine Albright stands out as a particularly influential figure in this narrative. Sec. Albright served as the U.S. Secretary of State from

1997 to 2001 under President Bill Clinton. During her tenure, one of the central focuses of U.S. foreign policy was the Middle East peace process, which included efforts to resolve the Israeli-Palestinian conflict. Jordan, being a key player in the region and having signed a peace treaty with Israel in 1994, was inevitably involved in many discussions and negotiations related to the peace process.

While Madeleine Albright was Secretary of State, the U.S. continued its strong support for Jordan, particularly after the death of King Hussein in 1999. Sec. Albright played a role in strengthening U.S.-Jordanian relations, emphasizing Jordan's role as a moderating influence in the Middle East.

After her tenure as U.S. Secretary of State, Madeleine Albright remained active in various capacities, including in relation to the Middle East. She transitioned from public service to roles in academia, private enterprise, and the nonprofit sector, which included the National Democratic Institute.

Sec. Albright served as the Chair of the National Democratic Institute (NDI) from 2001 until her passing in 2022. During her tenure, she brought extensive experience as a professor, author, diplomat, and businesswoman, including her service as the 64th Secretary of State of the United States. Her role at NDI was part of a distinguished career dedicated to promoting democracy, human rights, and good governance standards across the globe.

For those of us who were associated with NDI, she was an inspiration and a guiding light. She saw connections and relationships where others did not, and she provided unparalleled leadership, especially for women, at a time when it was not necessarily in vogue.

Madeleine Albright also co-founded the Albright Stonebridge Group, a global strategy firm affiliated with Dentons Global Advisors. Sec.

Albright's role in the group was very much in line with her distinguished career in diplomacy and international relations.

Although she was physically diminutive, Sec. Albright's presence was towering. She introduced innovative approaches during her tenure. She believed that while diplomats often operate within stringent guidelines—which are essential to maintain order—there are myriad conversations outside this framework that are important for a variety of reasons. These dialogues aren't exclusively with diplomats but extend to societal leaders, civil groups, political entities, engaged youth, and other key actors within a country or region.

Such discussions are vitally important because they help to pinpoint the root problems behind the thorniest of dilemmas. They also help identify common ground, foster unity, and increase the likelihood of finding solutions to those problems.

Albright's vision eventually gave rise to what's known today as "track-two diplomacy," which urges constructive engagement with both government officials and private groups and citizens. This concept, now widely practiced, was her brainchild.

One of Sec. Albright's initiatives was to enlist non-Americans to champion this form of diplomacy. For instance, in conflicts involving Romania, she'd engage individuals from other nations, those who had analogous experiences or could convey stories in specific contexts. Canadians, like myself, often found ourselves in roles where we could engage in dialogues that might be challenging for Americans.

Over the years, individuals from various countries, each with their unique histories and sets of experiences to share, have been recruited to participate in these efforts. This approach has facilitated diverse interactions, significantly influencing diplomatic efforts. Sec. Albright's enduring legacy in this realm is truly monumental.

Putting Optimize the Moment into Action

Diverse thinking is crucial when approaching a common problem. There will be natural leaders and distinct groups or tribes involved in the process, and within these tribes numerous factions will exist, each with their own agendas and influences.

Jordan is a monarchy, but it wishes its parliament and democracy to thrive, making it similar in some ways to the United Kingdom. The monarchy desires to remain unburdened by daily governance, leaving aspects like infrastructure and healthcare to the government. In this context, assisting political entities as they seek to improve their performance and helping the government establish better systems and communication channels can be highly impactful.

Whenever communication, negotiation, and resolution can be fostered, it's a step forward. While diplomats can sometimes facilitate these discussions, owing to their influence, there are moments when others can step in, unburdened by certain diplomatic protocols.

Something I experienced during my time in Jordan stands out as an example of both Optimize the Moment and relying on the community to make decisions and carry out the mission. As was the case in Indonesia and Ukraine, I had a young colleague who was helping me navigate the culture and customs and he was also my interpreter. He was invaluable.

He had an idea that I was initially very skeptical about, but he hadn't steered me wrong before. We kept trying to figure out how to pull some groups of people together to engage them in a project. He suggested that we should talk to a group of military veterans. My thought was that this approach wouldn't work because it was so far removed from what we were actually trying to achieve. I failed to see the connection or the value.

He reassured me, with that characteristic Jordanian smile, and made the call. The next thing I knew, we were driving for hours to a town in the northern part of the country.

The meeting was scheduled for nine in the morning, and I remember thinking, "Who'd show up so early on a weekend?" To add to the uncertainty, we were running late. Just a few minutes past our scheduled time, calls started coming in. "Where are you?" "Why the delay?" they'd ask. We explained our tardiness, due to traffic, and promised to be there soon.

To my astonishment, when we arrived, the place was packed. Everyone was punctual, and brimming with enthusiasm, and as I joked, they all had shiny shoes! Inside were about 50 retired military veterans.

I asked my colleague, "Did you tell them why we wanted to meet?" As we discussed the project and shared ideas, their drive was evident. Their motivation was boundless. Their nationwide connections became invaluable. This group, with their zeal and time at hand, was perfect for the task. Their willingness to help, without expecting any financial gains, made the whole experience remarkable. And yes, at every subsequent meeting they were punctual, and always wearing those ever-shiny shoes.

Upon the completion of our project, these veterans gave me a ring as a gift. They told me, "Whenever you're in Jordan, wear this." I expressed my gratitude, but my colleague clarified its significance.

"That ring," he said, "is more than just jewelry here." True to his words, whenever I approached a checkpoint or interacted with authorities, a glimpse of that ring would ensure my passage. Once again, I was deeply humbled.

From War Zones to Boardrooms: Some Observations

During my time at Merrill Lynch, there was a lot to admire about the company and how they ran their operations. When salespeople led the organization, the path to growth was clear. They saw the company as an organic entity, and they understood the interconnectedness of every department and every role. I learned a lot about synergies, collaboration, and the importance of a shared vision.

I have also witnessed organizations that were led by risk managers. While risk management is vital in the proper context, organizations can become too myopic when this concept becomes their primary focus. Often, cutting costs and resources are essential elements of business, but they cannot be the guiding philosophy for a growth-oriented company. The tactics they employ might seem rational in the short-term, but they are contrary to long-term mission development and implementation.

From my experiences in different countries, I've learned that community and culture are paramount. Individuals, regardless of their role, want to feel a sense of belonging, purpose, and value. People want to be a part of something bigger than themselves, this is essential to their motivation.

I have seen how the same applies with companies and other organizations. Whether it be in the C-suite or the various administrative levels, individuals play a crucial role in a company's ecosystem and want to feel like they have a sense of purpose (other than just making money).

I have seen the importance of having a clearly articulated mission, that people can see as a sense of purpose; a reason to get out of bed in the morning. It is something achievable, they can repeat it to others, and it helps to define their role in the organization. Achieving the mission means collective success and growth, and it means the satisfaction of achieving something together, sometimes with people who barely know each other but who come together as a team.

The organizations that get it right cultivate a sense of community within the company. People don't need to be best friends or share personal details to create an environment where they feel connected and valued, and where they look out for one another. There is tremendous confidence that comes from knowing your teammate has your back.

Short-term cost-cutting might boost quarterly reports, but there are numerous studies demonstrating the negative effects of "short-termism" on companies and even entire industries. For many of the reasons we have discussed already, decisions to offshore resources to save pennies per share in the current quarter may come back to haunt leaders when the world changes and new paradigms are required. Companies need leaders who can navigate the present while also steering the ship with a clear future destination in mind.

I have also observed that leadership styles need to adapt while being able to stay on mission. While risk management is essential, especially in certain situations, it should not be defined as a "mission" in itself. It is easy to get distracted and be pulled in different directions, especially when looking for shortcuts. Companies that demonstrate patience and a longer view are usually more successful.

Those on the front lines often know exactly what they are doing and what is needed to achieve the mission, which is why I always suggest to my clients that they ask the rank and file for their insights and opinions. Unfortunately, I see companies on a regular basis that have become too top down in their approach, as they try to put new plans into action with no input from those who are expected to implement them.

In my conversations with these neglected individuals, they give me highly informative feedback about why these top-down plans won't work, and they share with me what they would have suggested had they been asked. Usually, after a short period of following along, they forget about the plan and go back to doing what they were doing before, to keep food on the table and a roof overhead.

That would be classified as a "Missed Moment."

In contrast, leaders who regularly pay attention to those on the front lines, and who seek their opinions—especially contrary opinions—are those with the best-defined missions, with the greatest buy-in, and the best overall culture.

Leadership is hard. That's probably why there are so many books about it with people giving advice. I should probably say that Effective Leadership is hard, especially in these turbulent times where many of the rules have changed and the traditional tools used by leaders are no longer available or no longer apply.

The notion of "transparency," for example, is a relatively new concept that is so important to building trust. Not long ago, CEOs didn't care about being transparent with employees. They set the tasks and the targets and expected people to deliver. In a world where recruiting and retaining specific talent is increasingly difficult and important, transparency and building trust are key factors for success. Ethics come into play, but a distrusting workforce is less engaged, less productive, and more likely to suffer defections.

It's crucial for leaders to recognize and be sensitive to the current socioeconomic and political climate. Making drastic decisions without taking the broader implications into account can be disastrous.

The notion of things being irreparably broken and the need to find new ways of doing things is emblematic of our times. This reinforces the importance of adaptability and innovation in leadership. Being stuck in old patterns without recognizing when they are no longer viable is detrimental.

Leaders today need to be able to see things differently, and employ different models for decision-making, and for recruiting talent and keeping it. They should be able to discern which systems can be repaired and which need a complete overhaul.

At its core, leadership is about serving and uplifting others, ensuring that everyone is moving together toward a common goal. When leadership becomes about power or ego, it loses its essence. Leaders should always strive to remember their primary role: to be stewards of their organization and their people. It sounds obvious, but in practice it is not.

In times of unprecedented challenges, it is vital to rethink and update the playbook. We need new strategies, new tools, and innovative approaches to manage today's complexities. We are not going back to the "traditional world" we once knew.

The challenge, then, in today's crazy, mixed-up world, with all the geopolitical pushes and pulls and fundamental changes, is to create a corporate culture where every individual feels like a valued member of a team. Not just any team, but one where everyone is working together to achieve a common purpose, a mission that is definable, achievable, and worthwhile in the context of the greater good. When leaders and companies build such a culture, not only will they see financial growth, but they will also create a resilient, motivated, and innovative workforce capable of achieving great "moments."

Mission-Oriented Approach: The "How" Part

For me, the mission is one of the most important aspects of life, be it business or personal. Whether we're referring to being in a conflict zone—confronted with horrors and chaos—or working for a company, each person must know their role to complete the mission. And everyone's role is important.

There must be flawless (or near flawless) execution. Everyone involved must take ownership of the results for it to really work. This isn't articulated well in many companies—both small and large—but it needs to be. And companies that do involve all staff members execute their missions better than those that don't.

A mission (as distinct from a high level corporate "mission statement") isn't just words on a page. It clarifies, governs, and directs every move being made. Without a well-conceived mission, chaos ensues, and people's lives are often at stake as a result. And no, this isn't just hyperbole when you consider how quickly chaos can develop and how disruptive it can be.

Chaos … Happens

According to a Deloitte Center for Controllership poll published in 2023[6], during a recent 12-month period 34.5% of executives surveyed reported that their organizations' accounting and financial data had been targeted by cyber-attackers. Within that group, 22% experienced at least one such attack, while 12.5% experienced multiple intrusions. In addition, nearly half (48.8%) of C-suite and other executives polled expected the number and size of these cyber invasions to increase in the coming months. But despite these fears, only 20.3% of those polled said their organizations' accounting and finance teams were working closely and consistently with their companies' cyber-security departments.

Although this is not as common as a cyber-invasion, staff members or their family members can be targeted for kidnapping. And while this tends to happen most frequently in developing nations, such kidnappings have certainly been on the increase around the world over the past decade.

---

6   Almost Half of Executives Expect a Rise in Cyber Events Targeting Accounting and Financial Data in Year Ahead." 2 February 2023. SlideShare, https://www.slideshare.net/DeloitteUS/almost-half-of-executives-expect-a-rise-in-cyber-events-targeting-accounting-and-financial-data-in-year-ahead

At the macro level, wars and conflicts can spring up seemingly out of nowhere. Russia's invasion of Ukraine, the emergence of ISIS, the Arab Spring, the ongoing conflict between Palestine and Israel, and the Balkans Conflict are just a few such examples.

According to Blue Yonder Media Center's 2023 Supply Chain Executives Survey[7], which polled executives based in the United States, 87% of respondents reported experiencing supply chain disruptions within the past year. More than half (52%) of respondents cited customer delays as the most frequent outcome. Only six in 10 respondents (62%) indicated their supply chains were reliable enough to withstand the challenges of the present environment, meaning 38% were vulnerable.

Given the unpredictability of Mother Nature and the impacts of global warming, natural disasters can seemingly drop out of the sky. At the current time we are experiencing an increase in tornadoes and hurricanes[8], and in floods and fires. Although earthquakes can't be blamed on global warming, they can certainly devastate, and they can strike without warning.

Of course, a pandemic can develop out of nowhere, as we saw in 2020. Such an event can shut down the entire planet without notice. This is why I say that the mission should serve as the North Star during times when a company's operations are running smoothly, but especially when crises hit.

---

7   According to the Blue Yonder 2023 Supply Chain Executives Survey, which polled U.S.-based supply chain executives, 87% of respondents reported experiencing supply chain disruptions within the last year. More than half (52%) of respondents cited customer delays as the most frequent outcome. However, more than six in 10 respondents (62%) indicated their supply chains were reliable enough to withstand the pressure." Blue Yonder, 23 May 2022, https://media.blueyonder.com/blue-yonder-survey-finds-nearly-1-in-4-businesses-that-faced-supply-chain-disruptions/

8   NPR. 2023. "Why Hurricanes Feel Like They're Getting More Frequent." NPR, February 27, 2023. https://www.npr.org/2023/02/27/1158969044/why-hurricanes-feel-like-theyre-getting-more-frequent.

A mission-oriented approach in business represents a deliberate and unwavering commitment to a clear and purpose-driven objective that goes beyond mere money-making. It encapsulates a philosophy where an organization places its purpose at the forefront of its operations, decision-making processes, and planning.

At the core of a mission-oriented approach lies a well-defined and compelling statement of mission that serves as the driving force behind every action and initiative undertaken by the organization. A mission-oriented approach stands as the cornerstone of organizational success. This approach transcends traditional profit-centric models, instilling a deeper sense of purpose that guides every action and initiative within an organization.

Defining the mission provides clarity about the primary purpose or goal of the endeavor. It answers the fundamental question of "why" an organization exists, or explains why it is taking on a particular task.

But it goes much deeper than that. As someone who's navigated the complex intersection where leadership and strategy converge, I've often encountered confusion around the concept of a mission statement and the meaning of the mission itself within organizations.

A mission statement can be defined as a high-level goal, usually formulated with a view toward the horizon, or a focus on long-term results. It's a carefully crafted sentence or two that encapsulates what the organization does, whom it serves, and what makes it different. When I consult with a business, often the first thing I ask for is their mission statement, because it's supposed to provide a snapshot of their core purpose.

However, the mission represents a broader, more dynamic concept. It is defined by a clear, concise statement of the task of the unit and its purpose. While a mission statement is static, the mission is lived and experienced. It is not just written on a wall or website; it permeates every decision, strategic move, and interaction within the organization. The mission is a guiding force that influences the culture, objectives, and day-to-day operations of the company.

In my experience, the most successful organizations don't just have a mission statement. They also have a clear mission that is actively integrated into everything they do. It's one thing to say, "Our mission is to innovate and lead in our industry," and quite another to actually foster a culture of innovation and leadership. That's where the real differentiation lies.

When I consult with leaders and teams, I encourage them to not just create a mission statement, but to embody their mission daily. This means aligning their strategies, policies, and actions with the core purpose they've articulated. This is how you make the mission statement really mean what it says, as it becomes the heart and soul of the organization.

So, in summary, while a mission statement is a concise declaration of intent, the mission is the ongoing, living expression of that intent translated into action. It's the difference between stating a goal and actively pursuing it every day.

And that, in my experience, is what separates the good companies from the truly great ones.

Mission: It's Way More than a Statement

Let's look at the key aspects of what a mission-oriented approach includes and how implementing one can bode well for your company.

Organizations with a mission-oriented approach prioritize their mission's purpose above all else. Every business decision—from product development to market strategy—is evaluated through the lens of how it contributes to or aligns with the mission's goals. Profit is seen as a means to an end, with the end being the fulfillment of the mission.

The mission-oriented approach dovetails with the core values of the organization. These values guide ethical behavior, inform decision-making, and ensure that the organization's actions remain consistent with its mission. This arrangement fosters authenticity and trust with employees, customers, and stakeholders.

Organizations adopting this approach measure success not only by financial metrics, but also by the positive impact they create in the world. They set specific, measurable, and impactful goals related to their mission, whether it's environmental sustainability, social justice, or community empowerment. Progress toward these goals is regularly tracked and reported.

Mission-oriented organizations actively engage with their stakeholders, including employees, customers, suppliers, and the communities they serve. They seek input and feedback to ensure that their actions are in line with the needs and expectations of these groups. Collaboration and co-creation are encouraged to maximize the mission's reach and effectiveness.

As world events unfold, affecting everyone, organizations with a mission-oriented approach are adaptable and resilient. They remain agile, continuously learning and evolving their strategies to address new challenges and opportunities while staying true to their primary purpose.

Such organizations cultivate a culture that inspires and motivates employees. Team members are drawn to the organization not just for a paycheck, but because they believe in the mission and find meaning in their work. This sense of purpose drives high levels of engagement, innovation, and dedication among staff.

A mission-oriented approach is inherently focused on long-term sustainability. It seeks to create lasting change and positive outcomes that extend far into the future.

In essence, a mission-oriented approach transcends profit as the sole measure of success. It embodies a commitment to making a meaningful and enduring impact on society or a specific cause, recognizing that businesses have the potential to be powerful agents of positive change. This approach not only sets the organization apart but also resonates with individuals, customers, and partners who share a common passion for the mission's objectives. It's about recognizing that profit and purpose can coexist harmoniously, driving both financial success and societal betterment.

The Characteristics of a Galvanizing Mission

How can you, as a business owner, ensure your mission truly aligns with your goals while providing impact across the company and with everyone who depends on the company's success? From day-to-day operations to crises, a well-defined mission is crucial. Here are some things to think about as you carefully consider how to define your mission:

Your mission needs to serve as a guiding principle for decision-making. It will help determine which actions, strategies, and initiatives cohere with the overarching purpose, ensuring that choices are consistent with the mission goals.

A well-defined mission helps in focusing efforts and resources on what truly matters. It allows organizations or individuals to prioritize tasks and initiatives that contribute directly to the mission's achievement.

A clear mission can be a source of motivation and inspiration. It gives people a sense of purpose and a reason to work toward a common goal, fostering dedication and commitment.

When everyone involved understands and is focused on the mission, it promotes unity and teamwork. It ensures that everyone is working towards a shared objective, minimizing conflicts and promoting collaboration.

A defined mission creates a basis for accountability. It becomes possible to measure progress and success against the mission's objectives, helping to track performance and make adjustments as required.

A well-articulated mission can be effectively communicated to stakeholders, including employees, customers, partners, and the public. It helps in conveying the organization's purpose and values.

Defining the mission is a fundamental step in planning. It informs the development of strategies, goals, and action plans that are in harmony with the mission's overarching purpose.

The mission provides a stable point of reference, even in a changing environment. It allows organizations or individuals to adapt to new circumstances while remaining committed to their core purpose.

With a clear mission, it becomes possible to assess the impact of actions and initiatives. It helps in evaluating whether progress is being made toward fulfilling the mission, and also in evaluating the pace of that progress.

In summary, defining the mission is essential because it sets the direction, purpose, and framework for all subsequent activities. It ensures that efforts are purposeful, focused, and in accord with the all-encompassing goal, increasing the likelihood of success and mission fulfillment.

Now that you've learned about my background and about how and why I developed my Optimize the Moment concept, in the next section we'll begin focusing on implementation.

SECTION 2

Optimize the Moment:

A New Approach

Define the Mission

Before I jump into the "how to" portion of Define the Mission, I want to share a few thoughts about my "why."

In writing this book, I draw from a reservoir of unique experiences that have given me a distinct perspective on organizational effectiveness and human empathy. My journey through various roles, from empathetic missions to consulting for leading companies, has equipped me with insights into what truly works and what falls short in organizational dynamics.

This book is the culmination of these observations and experiences. It's about distilling the essence of effective leadership and impactful change — the kind that resonates on a deep, human level.

Through Optimize the Moment, I'm not just sharing theories. I'm also introducing bold, practical approaches that have shaped my understanding of success and leadership. From what I've observed, it is clear that the heart of every thriving organization is a core of empathy and understanding, and this book aims to bring that to the forefront.

Corporations excel in creating systems and structures that drive efficiency and innovation. They've harnessed technology and data to propel growth and stay competitive. Nevertheless, many fall short of fostering genuine empathy and understanding within their organizational culture. They often overlook the human element, which is the cornerstone of sustainable success.

My book is intended to be a call to action. As I said in my introduction, I hope to disrupt the way we do business, for the better. Optimize the Moment advocates for a transformative approach where empathy is as valued as efficiency. I believe that corporations can benefit from recalibrating their strategies, by recognizing that true excellence lies in balancing human-centric practices with operational prowess. This book is my contribution to an essential dialogue, as it represents a fusion of my experiences and a guide for those ready to make a meaningful change in the corporate landscape.

It's crucial to understand the foundation behind this book. My "why" stems from a career that spans from humanitarian missions to consulting with corporate leadership, giving me a multilayered perspective on what makes organizations tick. This book is a bold challenge to the corporate status quo, advocating for a balance between efficiency and empathy.

If I were to put my process for Optimizing the Moment in visual terms, it would look something like this:

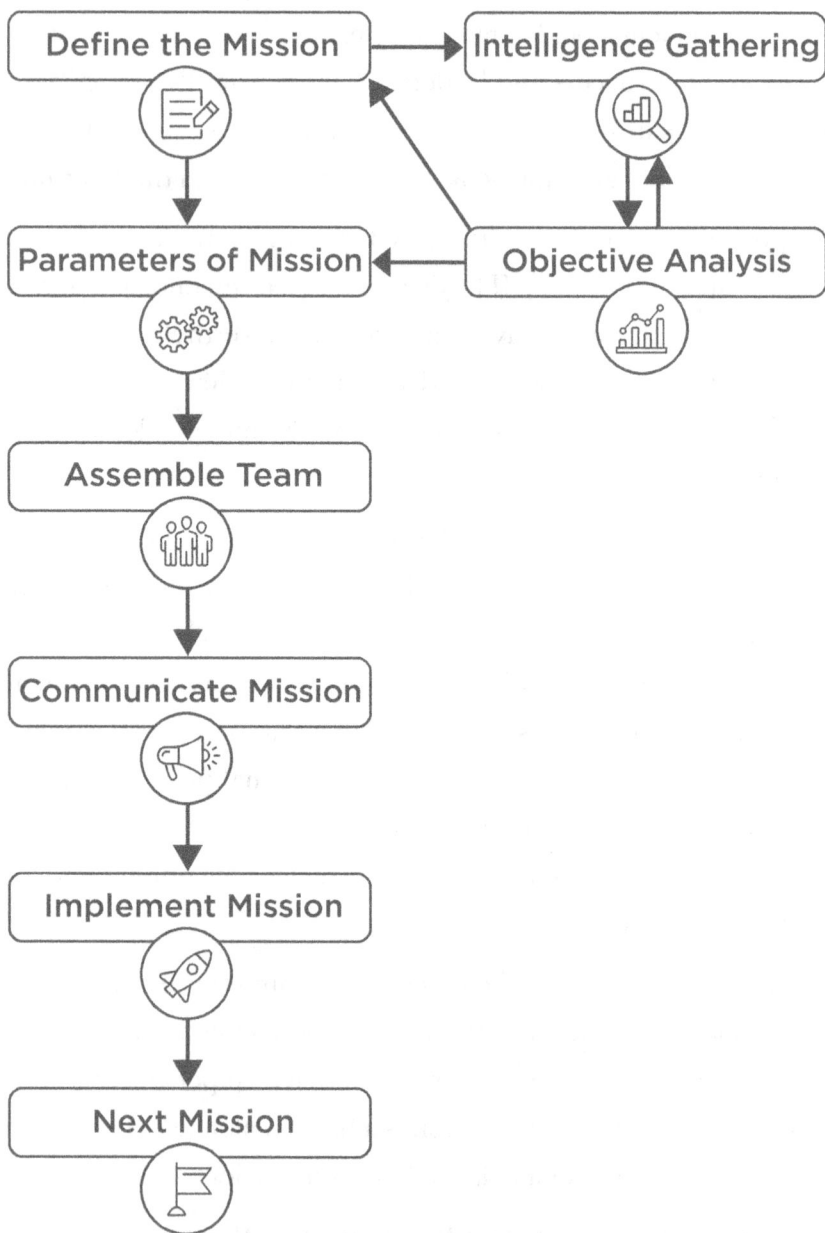

In general, it's linear, but as you'll see, sometimes things are happening simultaneously. At the moment, it may seem a little confusing, but as you read further, things will begin to take form and make sense.

Under the approach I'm recommending, when we embark on defining the mission we shouldn't just be setting a goal. We should be aligning with the core values that drive sustainable success and people-first business practices. This chapter will explore how to craft a mission that resonates deeply within an organization, guiding every decision toward achieving both operational excellence and meaningful impact.

In this chapter of Optimize the Moment, we'll look at what happens when you implement this approach. We'll look at every facet of the organization and how Optimize the Moment can improve the efficiency of your organization, while improving employee morale and providing next-level value to stakeholders and your customers.

Defining the mission is a foundational step in any endeavor, particularly in a business and organizational context. This means articulating a clear, compelling goal that guides every decision, objective, and action. Here, we delve into the nuances of defining a mission, exploring its various facets through a detailed examination.

However, before we commence with this task, let's briefly discuss both the mission and the mission statement, to see how they relate to business.

The Mission vs. Mission Statement

A common point of confusion in both military and corporate circles is differentiating between the Mission and a mission statement. While they might seem similar in name, their roles, impacts, and applications are distinctly different.

Mission Statement: The Theoretical Framework to Appease Stakeholders

Mission statements are often crafted to resonate with external stakeholders – shareholders, customers, and the public. They serve as a public-facing manifesto of an organization's values and aspirations. For instance, a mission statement promising "innovation for a better world" is designed to build confidence and support among investors, clients, and the market at large. While this is vital for brand image and investor relations, it often glosses over the practical realities faced by those who work within the organization.

A Disconnection with Employees

On the ground, employees – the ones who are tasked with bringing the Mission to life – might find the mission statement too abstract or disconnected from their daily challenges. While inspiring, the lofty ideals of a mission statement don't always translate into actionable guidance for employees. For them, the day-to-day operations, the nitty-gritty of the Mission, are what matter. Consequently, they need clear, achievable objectives, resources, and guidance on how their efforts contribute to the broader goals of the organization.

This is where the Mission comes into play. Unlike the broad strokes of a mission statement, the Mission is about actionable goals and strategies. It's the practical blueprint that employees follow – the specific campaigns, projects, or initiatives they're working on.

For example, while the mission statement might focus on broad goals like innovation, the Mission could involve developing a specific new product feature by a set deadline. This specificity is what employees require to understand their roles and responsibilities, and to know how their work fits into the larger picture.

The Impact of a Well-Defined Mission in Military Operations

The challenge for leaders is to bridge this gap, to ensure that the aspirational language of mission statements aligns with and informs the Mission. When employees understand how their work contributes to the broader aspirations of the organization, it fosters a sense of purpose and direction. Conversely, when mission statements are merely cosmetic, designed only to appease stakeholders without considering the practical implications for employees and the work they're expected to perform, it can lead to disillusionment and a lack of engagement.

By contrast, the Mission itself is dynamic, specific, and action oriented. It focuses on what we are doing right here, right now. The Mission is akin to a detailed battle plan in the military or a strategic business initiative in a corporate setting. It involves specific goals, defined timelines, and clear metrics for success.

In a military operation, the Mission could be to secure a specific village within a week, while keeping civilian disturbances to a minimum. In a business context, it might be launching a new product line by the end of the quarter, while ensuring quality is consistently baked into every aspect of what is being produced.

In the realm of military operations, the clarity and precision of the Mission are often the critical factors that determine success and mitigate casualties. Let's imagine a scenario in a conflict zone, which, while not drawn from my personal experience, encapsulates the pivotal role of a well-defined mission.

Hypothetical Operation: Rescue in a Conflict Zone

Consider a hypothetical military operation where the goal is to rescue hostages held in a volatile area where conflict has been ongoing. The area is known for its complex urban terrain, high civilian population, and aggressive enemy combatants.

In this scenario, the Mission is crystal clear: to rescue the hostages with minimal civilian casualties while ensuring that only the military personnel involved are aware of the Mission. This clarity is crucial. It informs every aspect of the operation, from the selection of the entry point, the timing of the raid, to the rules of engagement. The troops know exactly what is expected of them and the parameters within which they must operate.

As the operation unfolds, the troops move with precision and discipline. They are aware of the hostile environment but also of the need to minimize harm to civilians. Their training and the clarity of the Mission enable them to make split-second decisions that are in sync with the operation's objectives.

Contrast this with a scenario where the Mission is vague. Perhaps the objective is simply stated as 'neutralize the enemy threat.' Such ambiguity can lead to catastrophic outcomes, including lost soldiers, unintended civilian casualties, and potential harm to the hostages. Without a clear mission, soldiers might overstep, leading to a full-blown firefight that could have been avoided.

In our hypothetical operation, the disciplined approach, guided by a clear mission, leads to the successful rescue of the hostages with minimal collateral damage. This outcome is a direct result of the meticulous definition and understanding of the Mission.

The key difference lies in their application. A mission statement sets the overarching goal and ethos of the organization. It's what aligns every department and employee to a common purpose. The Mission, however, is about turning that purpose into tangible actions and measurable outcomes. It's the operationalization of the mission statement's ideals.

It's crucial to recognize that while distinct, the two concepts are not mutually exclusive. The Mission should always align with the broader ethos encapsulated in the mission statement. When an organization's missions are in harmony with its mission statement, it ensures coherence in strategy and purpose. This symbiosis is what drives successful outcomes, whether in a military operation or a corporate plan.

In my career, understanding and leveraging this distinction has been critical. The mission statement of my team or organization set our compass, but it was the Mission, and its tangible, actionable plans, that propelled us forward, allowing us to navigate through complexities and achieve concrete results.

Consequences of Not Having a Mission: Chaos Ensues

For American football fans, this scenario may be very familiar to you.

On December 30, 2023, the Georgia Bulldogs faced the Florida State Seminoles in the Orange Bowl. Before I get into the outcome and how it relates to the Mission, I first need to say that both teams were exceptional. There was nothing average about either team. As it relates to the Orange Bowl, Georgia demonstrated their Mission was better defined and executed.

Georgia's Implementation of a Clear Mission

Georgia's gameplay in the Orange Bowl demonstrated the power of a well-defined mission. From the outset, their strategy was clear: control the pace of the game, execute meticulously planned plays, and capitalize on the strengths of their key players. This clarity in mission allowed every player on the Georgia team to understand their role and how it would contribute to the success of the overarching strategy. As a result, their efforts on the field were coordinated, purposeful, and effective.

Florida State's Struggle Without a Defined Mission

Contrastingly, Florida State's performance suggested a lack of a similarly articulated mission. Without a clear strategic direction, players appeared to struggle to synchronize their efforts, leading to reactive rather than proactive gameplay. This lack of a unified mission resulted in disorganization, missed opportunities, and ultimately, a failure to effectively counter the strategies employed by Georgia.

The Outcome: A Reflection of Strategic Planning

The significant point differential (63-3) in favor of Georgia was not just a matter of athletic prowess; it was a testament to the impact of having a well-defined mission. Georgia's ability to implement their strategy effectively led to their dominant performance, while Florida State's apparent lack of a cohesive plan contributed to its overwhelming defeat.

Case Study of a Company with a Well-Defined and Articulated Mission: Apple Computers

In 1976, something extraordinary was started in a small garage in Cupertino, California. Three visionaries, Steve Jobs, Steve Wozniak, and Ronald Wayne, laid the foundation for Apple. This wasn't just about assembling computers; it was the beginning of a future that would reshape how we interact with technology.

The early years were like a scene from a classic underdog tale. The Apple I, a personal computer kit, was only the beginning. The 1980s saw Apple redefine the computing experience with the Apple II and then the Macintosh. These weren't just machines; they were gateways to a new world that was both user-friendly and innovative.

However, every story has its conflicts. The late 1980s and early 90s were challenging chapters for Apple. Internal struggles and rising competition tested the company's resolve. The plot took a dramatic turn when Steve Jobs, the visionary, departed. But as in every great story, the hero returns. In 1997, Jobs came back to Apple when it was on the brink, ready for transformation.

Then came the era of revolution. The year 2001 marked the launch of the iPod, which changed the music industry forever. In 2007, the world was introduced to the iPhone, a device that redefined communication. The iPad followed in 2010, and it quickly jumped to the top spot in the tablet market. These weren't just products; they were chapters in a story of world-transforming innovation.

The Essence, Communication, and Execution of Apple's Mission

Throughout this journey, Apple's mission was clear and resonant. They wanted to create an unparalleled user experience through innovation in hardware, software, and services. This mission was their beacon, guiding every decision and every creation.

Steve Jobs and his successors ensured that this mission was not just a statement, but a living ethos that defined Apple. It was communicated passionately to every employee, not just as a directive but as a shared dream. This clarity in mission empowered employees, helping them align their individual efforts with the company's grand narrative.

Every innovation at Apple reflected this mission. The meticulous design of the iPhone, the environmental initiatives, the unwavering focus on customer privacy and security—these were manifestations of a mission deeply ingrained in the company's culture.

The story of Apple is more than a corporate history. It's also a lesson in the power of a clear, shared purpose. It teaches us that when an organization's mission is understood and embraced by all, it becomes an unstoppable force. This tale isn't just about technology, but demonstrates how clarity of purpose can create a legacy that reshapes the world.

Defining the Mission: Putting it All into Context

Back in the introduction to this book, I introduced the idea of the Mission by stating, "Most problems in life are the result of poor communication. We all communicate every day and yet, it is something we rarely do well. Effective communication does not happen by default nor is it measured by quantity; brilliant communication is simple and clear."

Recalling what I said about the importance of empathy and purpose, Optimize the Moment is about building a solid team where each member's strengths are acknowledged and celebrated, and put to use for the good of the project. Everyone should know the mission and their role in it. Remember, it's not about the plan, but about each of our roles within the plan.

Looking at the two examples of the Orange Bowl and Apple, it's easy to see what happens when a Mission is clearly defined, articulated, and executed, and what happens when it is not.

Embracing Empathy in Corporate Missions

In my years consulting for various organizations, I've come to realize a fundamental truth often overlooked in the boardroom: at the core of every successful mission lies empathy. More than just an HR buzzword, empathy is the engine that drives sustainable success in today's corporate world.

Understanding Empathy Beneath the Surface

Empathy in business goes beyond understanding your employees and customers on a surface level. You must be able to truly step into their shoes and see the world through their eyes.

It's a profound connection that goes beyond mere data points or market research. Empathy means grasping the unspoken needs, the silent struggles, and the unarticulated aspirations of those you serve and work with each day.

Let's take a deeper look at how empathy transforms a corporate mission.

Imagine a company setting out to launch a new product. A traditional approach might focus solely on market share and profitability. But an empathy-driven mission goes further. It asks questions like: how does this product genuinely improve people's lives? Are we considering the diverse needs of our users? How can we make this accessible and beneficial to as many people as possible?

These are empathetic questions, and their impact on product development, and other aspects of business, can be profound.

Empathy in Leadership: My Personal Reflections

In my journey, I've led teams across different continents, from diverse cultural backgrounds. This experience taught me that empathy is not just understanding different perspectives, but authentically valuing them. Empathy compels you to create a workplace environment where every voice is heard and respected, and where the concerns of employees are addressed with as much seriousness as concerns over quarterly earnings.

When a mission is rooted in empathy, it creates a ripple effect throughout the organization. Employees feel more connected and motivated. They're not just showing up every day going through the motions for a paycheck, but instead, they have a purpose.

Customers sense this, too. They recognize when a company genuinely cares, and this builds loyalty that extends beyond any marketing campaign.

Empathy and Innovation: The Unseen Link

Empathy also fuels innovation. By understanding the real-world challenges of users, companies can develop solutions that truly matter. It's not innovation for the sake of innovation, it's innovation with a purpose.

For example, when designing a new app, an empathetic approach would involve considering accessibility features, ensuring it's usable for people with disabilities. This is a detail that might easily be overlooked with a profit-driven strategy.

Question about Defining the Mission

As a way to condense and clarify everything discussed in this chapter, here are some questions for you to ponder, broken down by subsection. These queries invite you to reflect on where you've been, and on where you might be able to go in the future:

1. Empathy in Action:

- Can you recall a situation where empathy made a significant difference in your professional decisions or actions?
- How can empathy be actively incorporated into everyday business practices and decision-making processes?

2. The Mission vs. Mission Statement:

- Reflect on your organization's mission statement. How does it align with the actual missions or projects undertaken by your team?
- What steps can be taken to ensure that the aspirational language of your organization's mission statement translates into practical, actionable goals?

3. Communication and Clarity:

- How effectively does your organization communicate its missions to all team members?
- What strategies can be employed to improve communication and understanding of the Mission across different levels of the organization?

4. Learning from Success and Failure:

- Reflecting on the Orange Bowl scenario, what lessons can be drawn about the importance of a clear, well-defined mission?

- How can the principles displayed by successful teams like Georgia's football squad be applied in your organizational context?

5. Empathy-Driven Innovation:

- Can you think of a product or service in your organization that could benefit from a more empathy-driven approach in its development or delivery?

- How can empathetic understanding of customers or clients lead to innovative solutions in your field?

6. Personal Leadership and the Mission:

- As a leader or team member, how can you contribute to defining and articulating the Mission in your workplace?

- What are some ways you can foster an environment where every voice is heard and every team member feels connected to the Mission?

Now, let's move on to a discussion of how the parameters of a Mission can be chosen and defined.

Define The Parameters
of the Mission

Defining the parameters of a mission involves establishing clear boundaries and guidelines within which the mission operates. This crucial step ensures that the mission's objectives are pursued effectively and efficiently, aligning with the overall strategy and values of the organization.

Here are 10 recommendations on how to proceed:

1. You can develop an outline that explains in clear language what is included in the mission and, equally importantly, what is not. This approach will help you prevent mission creep and make it easier for your team to focus on the core objectives.

2. Knowing what you know about your company's current capabilities, you can determine what resources are available for a particular mission, including budget, personnel, technology, and time. This will help you set realistic expectations, and aids in effective planning.

Optimize the Moment

3. As a precautionary step, it can be a good idea to identify potential risks and challenges that could impact the mission. This will help you devise strategies to mitigate these risks, ensuring the mission remains on track despite any unforeseen obstacles you might encounter.

4. In consultation with colleagues, you can try to determine who needs to be involved or informed about the mission. This list of people could include team members, partners, customers, and other stakeholders who might be impacted by or can influence the mission.

5. It could be helpful to establish some clear criteria for what success looks like. This would most likely include specific, measurable outcomes that indicate the mission's objectives have been achieved.

6. You should strive to set a realistic timeline for the mission, including key milestones and deadlines. This helps in tracking progress and maintaining momentum.

7. While it's important to have clear parameters, you should also have built-in flexibility so you can adapt to changing circumstances or new information.

8. You'll probably want to double check to make sure the mission's parameters are aligned with legal requirements and your ethical standards. This is crucial for maintaining integrity and public trust.

9. It could be wise to implement mechanisms for ongoing feedback and communication within the team and with stakeholders. This allows for continuous improvement and adjustments of the mission's parameters as needed.

10. As the final step, you can plan for regular evaluation and review of the mission's parameters. This ensures that they remain relevant and effective over time.

If you incorporate these elements into the process of defining the parameters of a mission, you'll likely find it provides a robust framework that guides decision-making, ensures alignment with broader organizational goals, and facilitates successful mission execution.

How Purpose Functions in the Mission

Organizations that embrace purpose-driven actions prioritize the fulfillment of their mission as the ultimate goal. This means that every significant decision, whether it pertains to product development, market expansion, or resource allocation, is made with a deep consideration of how it matches and advances the mission's objectives.

When evaluating business strategies or initiatives, leaders and teams assess them through the lens of mission alignment. They ask critical questions such as, "How does this initiative contribute to our mission's core purpose?" and "Will it help us make a meaningful impact in the areas our mission addresses?" This holistic evaluation ensures that each action resonates with the mission's values and goals.

In this approach, profit is not an end in itself, but a means to achieve the mission's purpose. While profitability remains important for sustainability and growth, it is viewed as a tool that enables organizations to amplify their impact and extend their reach. Profit is reinvested to further the mission, rather than being solely reserved for personal gain or shareholder dividends.

Here are some of the defining characteristics of missions that are motivated first and foremost by purpose:

Purpose-driven actions require organizations to respect and account for the values and expectations of their stakeholders. This includes customers, employees, investors, and the wider community. By demonstrating a commitment to shared values, organizations can build trust and loyalty among their stakeholders.

In sharp contrast to an exclusive focus on profit, purpose-driven actions promote a long-term perspective in decision-making. Rather than focusing on short-term gains, organizations with a mission-oriented approach recognize that fulfilling their mission often requires sustained effort and a vision that focuses on future goals. This outlook encourages patience and persistence in pursuing meaningful change.

Purpose-driven organizations often prioritize social and environmental responsibility as integral components of their mission. They acknowledge their role in addressing pressing societal and environmental challenges, and they take proactive steps to minimize negative impacts while maximizing positive contributions.

Employees in organizations that prioritize purpose-driven actions tend to be more engaged and satisfied with their work. They see their daily efforts as contributing to a greater cause, which can boost morale and motivation. This sense of purpose can attract and retain talent who share the organization's commitment to the mission.

Purpose-driven organizations tend to be more resilient and adaptable. They are better equipped to weather challenges and disruptions because their commitment to their mission transcends short-term setbacks. This resilience allows them to pivot, innovate, and find creative solutions to any obstacles that might arise.

Case Study: Tesla's Mission in Action: Sustainable Innovation and Disaster Response

Before we get into this case study, let's look a little closer at what Tesla actually does.

Tesla, Inc. produces electric vehicles (EVs) and is focused on clean energy. The company was founded by Elon Musk and JB Straubel in 2003. It is named after the brilliant and eclectic inventor Nikola Tesla, and is headquartered in Palo Alto, California. Tesla is known for its innovative electric cars, including the Model S, Model 3, Model X and Model Y, as well as electrical energy products like solar panels and energy storage solutions (batteries).

If you know of Tesla only in relation to EVs, you may not realize that their solar panels are widely used. Tesla produces state-of-the-art solar panels for residential installations, allowing homeowners to generate clean energy from the sun and reduce their reliance on traditionally generated electricity. Many businesses and commercial properties have installed Tesla solar panels on their rooftops as well, to reduce energy costs and lower their environmental impact. Tesla's energy storage product, the Powerpack battery system, has been used in various locations to store excess solar energy for later use, or to provide backup power during grid outages.

Perched forever on the cutting edge, Tesla has also been involved in large-scale solar farm projects, which are used to generate renewable energy on a massive scale. These solar farms typically supply electricity to the grid instead of to individual customers. Tesla has also partnered with utility companies to develop utility-scale energy storage projects that help stabilize the electrical grid and increase the use of renewable energy sources. Tesla's solar panels and energy storage solutions have been integrated into microgrid systems, providing localized and resilient power generation and distribution in areas with unreliable grid infrastructure.

Tesla's solar products are also used in off-grid and remote locations, such as remote research stations, islands, and isolated communities, to provide reliable and sustainable energy sources.

While its primary founder remains a controversial figure, there is no doubt that Tesla has enjoyed astounding success in the renewable energy and green technology sectors.

Tesla's Response During Crisis: Testimony to its Mission in Real Time

Not much has been written about the role Tesla played in the rebuilding of Puerto Rico's power grid following Hurricane Maria in September 2017. All of Puerto Rico's powerlines are above ground and after 24 hours of category 4 winds (209 to 251 kmh/130 mph to 156 mph) and torrential rains, the entire grid was destroyed, along with three-quarters of the telephone poles and power lines. In the wake of this carnage, homes, small businesses being without power, hospitals, and all government buildings were without power.

The rebuilding effort took more than a year to complete. Some towns saw the restoration of power after a month. Most received power within seven to eight months. A handful didn't see power for up to 14 months.

Tesla responded swiftly to this crisis, and has continued to work with Puerto Rico, a United States commonwealth, to improve its power grid. Tesla collaborated with the Puerto Rican government and local authorities to identify areas where its solar and energy storage solutions could be most effective in restoring power and improving energy resilience. They installed solar panels and energy storage systems, including Powerpacks and Powerwalls, in various locations on the island to create microgrids, which can act as supplements to or replacements for the traditional electrical grid.

One of their more notable projects involved the installation of solar panels and energy storage systems at the Hospital del Niño (Children's Hospital) in San Juan. This installation was intended to provide a reliable source of electricity to the hospital, and it proved critical for providing medical services.

Tesla also worked on projects to bring solar power to communities and to critical facilities in Puerto Rico that were heavily impacted by the hurricane. These initiatives aimed to reduce dependence on traditional fossil fuel generators and increase the use of clean energy from renewable energy sources.

Just a few weeks after the hurricane, in October 2017, Tesla CEO Elon Musk publicly expressed the company's willingness to help Puerto Rico rebuild its energy infrastructure using solar power and energy storage technology.

Tesla's initial response, which included discussions and offers of assistance, began within weeks of the hurricane's impact. However, the actual implementation of specific projects and installations took some time to coordinate and execute, given the complexity of the situation and the need for careful planning and collaboration with local authorities. Tesla's involvement in Puerto Rico continued over the following months, with various solar and energy storage projects being initiated to enhance the island's energy resilience.

Tesla's efforts in Puerto Rico were part of its broader mission to promote clean energy development everywhere. Their involvement in Puerto Rico highlighted the potential for renewable energy and energy storage technologies to play a constructive role in disaster recovery, and to help create more resilient energy systems as a hedge against the impact of extreme weather events. Even after its initial emergency response, Tesla continued to work on projects to enhance energy infrastructure and provide sustainable solutions for the island, while also striving to raising awareness about the importance of transitioning to sustainable and environmentally friendly energy sources.

I purposely chose Tesla for this case study because of the clarity and purpose behind its mission, which motivates its work not just in its day-to-day operations, but also during crises. Tesla's response time to Puerto

Rico's emergency was swift and its approach organized, which enabled it to provide significant real-time relief. Without a well-defined and correctly conceived mission, Tesla never would have been able to move this rapidly or in such a well-coordinated fashion.

Tesla's Mission Statement and Mission

In addition to their impressive work in solar energy, Tesla has been a pioneer in advancing EV technology, with a focus on increasing the range of electric vehicles, improving battery efficiency, and developing autonomous driving capabilities. The company's electric cars have gained popularity for their performance, long-range capabilities, and cutting-edge features. Tesla's Autopilot system represents a significant step forward in the quest for reliable autonomous driving technology.

Over the years, Tesla has become one of the most valuable and influential companies in the automotive and clean energy industries, sparking significant changes in the transportation and energy sectors.

So how have they managed to accomplish so much?

For starters, Tesla, Inc. has a well-defined and provocative mission statement, which is "to accelerate the world's transition to sustainable energy." Tesla's mission statement serves as a North Star for the company's efforts at innovation. It clarifies that their primary purpose is not just to manufacture electric vehicles, but to drive a broader transition to sustainable energy solutions. This clarity guides the development of their electric cars, solar products, and energy storage solutions, products that all adhere to the demands of their mission statement.

Tesla's mission statement provides a clear and compelling purpose for the organization's existence. But to understand the importance of the mission in context with the mission statement, it must be pointed out that the way Tesla operates aligns with the principles of Mission Command.

Tesla has a well-defined and publicly stated mission that guides its overall strategy and product development. They are known for encouraging innovation and creativity among their employees, leaving them free to actualize the mission in a variety of ways. Their creative work has led to significant advancements in electric vehicle technology, battery storage, and other areas related to sustainable energy.

Tesla's approach is highly adaptive, focusing on quick iteration and responsiveness to challenges and opportunities, which is a key aspect of the Mission Command approach. Famed Tesla CEO Elon Musk is known for his visionary style and has often empowered his team to make critical decisions that he knows will ultimately align with the company's mission.

Tesla's mission has not only influenced its internal operations, but has also impacted the broader automotive and energy industries, helping to drive the global shift toward sustainability. In addition, it inspires its employees. Team members are motivated by the idea of working for a company that is actively contributing to a more sustainable future. They understand the "why" behind what they do, which fosters dedication and a sense of purpose and meaning.

Always striving for full transparency, Tesla makes sure it communicates its mission to all stakeholders, including customers, investors, and the public. It helps these stakeholders understand the broader purpose behind Tesla's products and services, emphasizing the company's commitment to sustainable energy.

The mission statement provides a basis for measuring impact. Tesla can assess its progress in accelerating the world's transition to sustainable energy by evaluating factors such as the global adoption of electric vehicles, the deployment of solar panels, and the reduction of carbon emissions.

Alignment with Values in a Mission-Oriented Approach: The Benefits

In the context of a mission-oriented approach, alignment with values represents a cornerstone principle that guides an organization's ethical behavior, decision-making, and overall conduct. It emphasizes the fundamental connection between an organization's mission and its core values, fostering authenticity, trust, and a sense of purpose up and down the roster.

Core values are the foundational principles that reflect an organization's deeply held beliefs, ethics, and standards. In a mission-oriented approach, these core values serve as guiding lights that influence every aspect of the organization's operations. They provide a moral compass for decision-making and behavior.

Alignment with values ensures that the organization's actions and decisions consistently adhere to its ethical standards. It means that ethical considerations are integral to the decision-making process, and leaders prioritize moral responsibility in their choices.

The alignment of values with the mission is essential to maintaining a coherent and purposeful organizational ethos. It ensures that the organization's actions and initiatives are not only ethical but also directly support and reinforce the mission's overarching purpose and objectives.

When an organization coordinates its actions with its values and mission, it projects authenticity to its stakeholders, including employees, customers, and partners. This authenticity breeds trust, as stakeholders can rely on the organization to live up to its commitments and promises.

Employees in organizations that prioritize alignment with values often feel a stronger connection to their work. They identify with the organization's values and mission, which can enhance their job satisfaction, motivation, and commitment.

Customers are more likely to trust and remain loyal to organizations that demonstrate a consistent alignment with values and mission. When customers perceive that a company's values resonate with their own, they are more inclined to support the business and its products or services.

Alignment with values extends to relations with stakeholders, including investors, suppliers, and local communities. Organizations that consistently demonstrate their commitment to shared values build confidence among these stakeholders, which can lead to stronger partnerships and collaborations.

Ethical leadership is a natural outcome of an uncompromising focus on values. Leaders within an organization will serve as role models by upholding the values that inspire the mission in all of their actions and decisions. This, in turn, sets a positive tone for the entire company or agency.

Organizations with a strong alignment with values are often more resilient in times of crisis. Their ethical foundations provide a stable platform from which to navigate challenges and make difficult decisions, while also allowing them to emerge from troubled times with their reputations intact.

Alignment with values supports long-term sustainability by fostering a corporate culture that emphasizes the primacy of ethical conduct, responsible practices, and a commitment to making a positive impact on society and the environment.

When incorporated into a mission-oriented approach, an alignment with values will act as a powerful force that not only defines an organization's character, but also strengthens its relationships with stakeholders and reinforces its commitment to its mission. It transforms the organization into a trusted, purpose-driven entity that strives for ethical excellence in all its endeavors.

Impact-Centric Approach in a Mission-Oriented Context

An impact-centric approach in a mission-oriented context signifies a fundamental shift in how organizations measure and prioritize success. Rather than solely relying on financial metrics, impact-centric organizations place a significant emphasis on the positive outcomes and changes they create, all of which are anticipated as a natural consequence of their missions. This shift goes beyond profit and strives for meaningful, measurable, and positive impacts on society, the environment, or a specific cause.

Here's what it means to be impact-centric from an organizational sense:

Impact-centric organizations redefine their success metrics. While financial performance remains important, it is complemented by a comprehensive set of impact indicators that reflect the organization's mission. These indicators may include reductions in carbon emissions, improvements in social equity, or advancements in community well-being.

To quantify their commitment to impact, organizations set specific, measurable and achievable goals related to their mission. These goals are well-defined, allowing for clear tracking and evaluation of progress. They provide a roadmap for the implementation of the mission's objectives.

Each objective and key result within the organization is tied directly to the mission's purpose and impact goals. This alignment ensures that every action taken, whether it's product development, market expansion, or community engagement, contributes meaningfully to the mission.

Progress toward impact goals is not a one-time effort. Rather, it's an ongoing commitment. Impact-centric organizations routinely track and report their performance as measured against these goals. Regular reporting ensures transparency and accountability to stakeholders, including employees, customers, and investors.

An impact-centric approach encourages organizations to continuously improve their impact strategies. If certain goals are not met or if new opportunities arise, organizations adapt and refine their strategies to maximize their positive contributions.

Impact-centric organizations conduct holistic assessments of their impact. They consider not only the direct effects of their actions, but also the potential ripple effects and unintended consequences. This comprehensive perspective helps avoid negative externalities.

Stakeholders play a crucial role in impact-centric organizations. They are involved in goal-setting, progress monitoring, and decision-making processes. Engaging stakeholders ensures that impact goals are aligned with their expectations and needs.

Impact-centric organizations ensure that their impact efforts fully harmonize with the core values of their mission in every instance. This harmonization reinforces the authenticity of their commitment and fosters trust among stakeholders.

Transparency is a key principle in impact-centric organizations. They openly share their impact data, including successes and challenges, with stakeholders. Accountability mechanisms are in place to address any deviations from impact goals.

Organizations with an impact-centric approach take a long-term perspective. They recognize that meaningful impact often requires sustained effort and a commitment to enduring change.

An impact-centric approach within a mission-oriented context represents a visionary commitment to making a tangible difference in the world. It transcends the traditional focus on profit by prioritizing specific, measurable, and positive impacts on society, the environment, or a chosen cause. Such organizations not only contribute to their mission's purpose, but also foster a culture of social responsibility and ethical leadership that resonates with employees, customers, and stakeholders alike. They are at the forefront of social change, and are admired for that.

Stakeholder Engagement in Mission-Oriented Organizations

Stakeholder engagement is a fundamental principle within mission-oriented organizations. They emphasize active and meaningful interaction with all relevant parties involved in or impacted by the organization's activities. This approach recognizes the interconnectedness of various stakeholders, including employees, customers, suppliers, and the communities served, and strives to customize the organization's actions to meet everyone's needs and expectations.

Stakeholder engagement implies a deep commitment to social unity and interpersonal harmony, as it demonstrates through the following characteristics:

Mission-oriented organizations adopt an inclusive approach to stakeholder engagement, acknowledging that a diverse range of perspectives and interests exist among their stakeholders. They actively seek to involve all relevant parties in decision-making processes.

Stakeholder engagement involves soliciting input and feedback from stakeholders on various aspects of the organization's activities, including its mission, strategies, products, and services. This feedback loop allows for a better understanding of stakeholder needs and concerns.

Collaboration and co-creation are encouraged in mission-oriented organizations. They view stakeholders as partners in achieving the mission's objectives. By working collaboratively, organizations can tap into the collective knowledge and creativity of stakeholders to develop more effective solutions.

Mission-oriented organizations prioritize alignment with the values and expectations of their stakeholders. They strive to ensure that their actions and decisions resonate with the values and interests of their employees, customers, and the communities they serve.

Transparency is a cornerstone of stakeholder engagement. Organizations openly communicate their intentions, actions, and progress to stakeholders. This transparency builds trust and accountability and ensures that stakeholders are well-informed.

Stakeholder engagement is viewed as necessary for the creation of mutually beneficial relationships. Organizations recognize that by meeting the needs and expectations of stakeholders, they can enhance their own success and impact. This perspective fosters long-term, symbiotic partnerships.

Mission-oriented organizations actively engage with the communities in which they operate. They seek to understand local dynamics, contribute positively to community well-being, and address any potential negative impacts.

Employees play a vital role in stakeholder engagement. Mission-oriented organizations empower employees to participate in decision-making processes and encourage them to voice their ideas and concerns. Engaged employees are more committed to the mission, this is an inevitable benefit of this approach.

Organizations that engage with stakeholders are more adaptable and responsive to changing circumstances and evolving stakeholder needs. This adaptability allows them to stay true to their missions while remaining agile in the face of challenges.

Stakeholder engagement is an ongoing process. Mission-oriented organizations continuously seek ways to improve their engagement practices, ensuring that they remain relevant and effective.

What it all boils down to is that stakeholder engagement is a vital component of mission-oriented organizations. It is rooted in the belief that meaningful change and mission fulfillment require collaboration, open communication, and shared commitment with all stakeholders. By actively engaging with their employees, customers, suppliers, and communities, these organizations not only enhance their impact, but also foster a culture of trust, accountability, and social responsibility that permeates their operations.

Adaptability and Resilience in Mission-Oriented Organizations

Adaptability and resilience are key attributes of organizations that embrace a mission-oriented approach. In a world marked by constant change and uncertainty, these organizations prioritize the ability to adapt to evolving circumstances while remaining steadfast in their commitment to their mission and purpose.

Mission-oriented organizations understand that strategies must be flexible and responsive to external changes. They are willing to adjust their approaches, tactics, and plans when new challenges or opportunities arise. This adaptability enables them to seize opportunities and mitigate threats effectively.

Meanwhile, a culture of continuous learning is cultivated within these organizations. They encourage employees to seek new knowledge, stay updated on industry trends, and adapt to evolving best practices. This commitment to learning ensures that the organization remains innovative and forward-thinking.

Innovation is not just an occasional event, but a fundamental aspect of the organizational culture. Mission-oriented organizations encourage employees to propose and experiment with innovative solutions to address emerging issues or enhance the impact of their mission.

Rather than simply reacting to change, these organizations proactively anticipate change and trends. They conduct scenario planning and risk assessments to identify potential disruptions and develop strategies to address them.

Mission-oriented organizations are resilient in the face of adversity. They understand that setbacks and challenges are part of the journey, but they remain committed to their mission despite difficulties. Their boundless resilience allows them to bounce back from setbacks and continue their work.

The organization's mission serves as a guiding light that helps maintain focus during times of change. It provides a constant reference point for decision-making, ensuring that adaptations remain aligned with the organization's core purpose.

Employees are encouraged to share insights, propose changes, and collaborate on strategies to address evolving challenges. This sense of ownership and empowerment boosts the organization's collective ability to adapt.

Transparent and effective communication is essential. Leaders communicate changes, challenges, and adaptation strategies clearly to employees and stakeholders, maintaining trust and confidence in the organization's ability to anticipate and manage change.

Mission-oriented organizations engage in scenario planning to anticipate various future scenarios and develop contingency plans. This proactive approach enables them to respond swiftly and effectively to unexpected events.

Risk management is integral to adaptability and resilience. These organizations assess risks systematically and implement risk mitigation measures to protect their mission and stakeholders.

Flexibility and durability are fundamental to the success of mission-oriented organizations. They enable these organizations to thrive in a rapidly changing world by remaining agile and learning from experience, and they learn to embrace innovation as their calling card. The mission acts as a constant point of reference, guiding decision-making and ensuring that adaptations continue to reflect the organization's core values and purpose.

Through all the attributes just listed, mission-oriented organizations are better equipped to fulfill their missions, create positive impacts, and endure in the face of uncertainty.

Inspiring Culture in Mission-Oriented Organizations

An inspired and inspiring culture are hallmarks of mission-oriented organizations. These organizations intentionally strive to create and support an environment where employees are not just motivated by financial compensation, but feel deeply connected to the organization's mission and find profound meaning in their work. This sense of purpose ignites high levels of involvement, creativity, and unwavering dedication among staff.

Acting as a source of both illumination and inspiration, the organization's mission is at the heart of its culture. It serves as a unifying force that links the actions and values of employees to the organization's ultimate purpose, in a virtuous relationship that ensures the mission will have the broadest possible impact.

A close analysis of how inspirational organizations work would reveal the following traits:

Mission-oriented organizations cultivate shared values and beliefs that have deep meaning for their employees. These values create a sense of belonging and unity, reinforcing the common purpose that unites the team.

Employees in these organizations find personal and professional fulfillment in their roles. They understand how their contributions directly contribute to the mission's objectives, leading to a sense of pride and accomplishment.

Leadership within mission-oriented organizations is characterized by an inspirational approach. Leaders lead by example, demonstrating unwavering commitment to the mission and its values. They inspire and empower employees to bring their best selves to work, and to stretch their wings in pursuit of the noblest possibilities.

In an inspirational working culture open communication is prized, as employees are encouraged to share their thoughts, ideas, and concerns. This transparent environment fosters trust and a spirit of collaboration.

As true stakeholders, employees are empowered to take ownership of their work and contribute to the mission's success. They have autonomy and are encouraged to think outside the box and to seek solutions independently.

An inspirational workplace culture rejects and transcends the traditional paradigm, where employees are too often conceived as secondary contributors merely seeking a weekly paycheck. As an alternative, mission-oriented organizations purposefully cultivate an environment where employees are intricately linked to the very essence of the organization's purpose, as respected contributors and even as co-creators.

Respect for the talent and wisdom of employees and staff extends beyond the confines of a job description; it delves into the heart and soul of an organization's purpose. When employees find themselves embedded in a culture brimming with a profound sense of purpose, they experience a unique form of motivation that goes beyond that offered via monetary rewards.

This profound sense of purpose becomes the driving force behind their daily efforts, which is reflected in their enthusiasm and dedication. They don't perceive their tasks as responsibilities, but as meaningful contributions to a greater cause. As a result, their engagement levels soar, and they become active participants in the organization's mission, rather than passive bystanders.

When employees feel deeply connected to the mission, they become deeply invested in the organization's success. This emotional commitment prompts them to fearlessly and proactively seek innovative solutions, as they are more willing to go the extra mile to overcome challenges. They tap into their creativity, pushing boundaries to find novel approaches that really work.

Furthermore, this sense of connection fosters a strong sense of belonging and camaraderie among employees. They understand they are part of something bigger than themselves, and this realization strengthens their bonds with their colleagues. In this interconnected ecosystem, employees are not just co-workers, but allies on a shared quest.

When employees are more connected to an organization's mission, they feel empowered to show up every day, They do this not out of obligation, but out of a genuine desire to contribute to a worthwhile cause. This empowerment fuels their commitment, enhances their creativity, and fosters a collaborative spirit, ultimately driving the organization toward its mission-driven goals with unwavering intent and dedication.

An Inspirational Culture as the Exception Rather than the Rule

Unfortunately, only 23% of U.S. employees feel engaged enough in their company's mission to see themselves as co-contributors or co-creators. This is according to a Gallup survey taken in 2022[9].

Clearly, there is room for improvement.

In contrast to companies that don't concern themselves with inspiring their employees, mission-oriented organizations value and appreciate the efforts of their staff members and other workers, and aren't reluctant to let them know it. Recognition programs acknowledge and celebrate their achievements and contributions to the mission, reinforcing a sense of shared purpose.

A commitment to continuous learning and development is embedded in the culture. Employees are encouraged to develop new skills and expand their knowledge, which will enable them to excel in their roles and contribute more effectively to the mission.

Employees are highly engaged in their work, due to their strong connection to their assignments. They are emotionally invested in the organization's success and are motivated to go above and beyond to achieve its goals.

An inspiring culture respects innovation and creativity, regardless of the source. Employees are encouraged to think outside the box and propose new ideas and approaches that can advance the mission.

Staff members in these organizations exhibit a deep commitment to their roles. They are willing to put in extra effort because they believe in the cause and are driven by a motivating sense of purpose.

---

9   Gallup. 'Employee Engagement.' Gallup, https://www.gallup.com/394373/indicator-employee-engagement.aspx

Strong interpersonal relationships are nurtured within the mission-oriented organization. Employees support and uplift one another, creating a positive and collaborative work environment.

An inspiring culture within mission-oriented organizations is a powerful force that fuels employee enthusiasm, engagement, and dedication. It transforms the workplace into a vibrant and purpose-driven community where employees are not only drawn to their roles, but are also committed to making a meaningful impact in the world. This culture is a driving force behind the organization's ability to fulfill its mission and create positive change in society.

Long-Term Sustainability in Mission-Oriented Organizations

Long-term sustainability is a fundamental principle in mission-oriented organizations. These organizations are inherently committed to ensuring not only their own continued viability, but also the enduring sustainability of their mission's impact. Their focus extends beyond immediate results, aiming to create lasting change and positive outcomes that extend far into the future.

Sustainability begins with a mission-centric approach. The organization's mission serves as a guiding light that directs its actions and strategies over the long term. It provides a sense of purpose that transcends short-term goals.

Mission-oriented organizations engage in planning that spans years or even decades. They develop roadmaps that outline how they will achieve their mission over the long haul, with a special focus on remaining adaptable and resilient in the face of changing circumstances.

These organizations are prudent stewards of resources, both financial and non-financial. They carefully manage their assets to ensure they can continue to operate and advance their mission well into the future.

Significant portions of resources are allocated to advancing the mission. These organizations prioritize investing in initiatives and projects that create sustainable, long-lasting impact rather than short-term gains. Of course, they know that the former will eventually produce the latter, which puts them ahead of the curve in comparison to their more short-sighted competitors.

Long-term sustainability is monitored through the measurement of impact over time. Mission-oriented organizations track and assess the enduring effects of their actions, ensuring that they are making progress toward their long-term goals.

Recognizing that the world is dynamic and ever-changing, these organizations remain flexible, or light on their feet. They are prepared to adjust their strategies and tactics to remain relevant and effective in the face of evolving challenges and opportunities.

Long-term sustainability often relies on collaborations and partnerships. Mission-oriented organizations engage with other entities, including governments, NGOs, and communities, to amplify their impact and tackle complex, systemic issues.

Ensuring the continuity of the organization's mission involves succession planning. Organizations identify and prepare new leaders who can carry the mission's torch and values forward into the future.

Long-term sustainability also includes the concept of legacy-building. Mission-oriented organizations strive to leave a legacy of positive change in the areas they address, even after their direct involvement has concluded.

These organizations prioritize ethical and responsible practices in all aspects of their work. They recognize that ethical behavior is essential for building trust and maintaining long-term credibility.

Some mission-oriented organizations actively engage with younger generations to instill a sense of responsibility and commitment to the mission. This engagement helps ensure that the mission remains relevant and sustainable over time.

Long-term sustainability is a core value and strategic imperative within mission-oriented organizations. They are driven by a deep commitment to creating lasting change and positive outcomes that endure far into the future. By maintaining a focus on their mission, responsible resource management, and adaptability, these organizations are well-positioned to fulfill their missions for generations to come, leaving an indelible impact on society and the world.

In conclusion, we underscore the essence of mission-oriented organizations: their steadfast dedication to purpose-driven actions. This commitment transcends mere profitability, focusing instead on creating substantial, positive impacts that align with core values and the broader mission.

These organizations embody resilience, adaptability, and an unwavering focus on long-term sustainability, thus ensuring their actions resonate deeply with stakeholders and contribute to meaningful societal change.

As we transition to the next chapter, we'll explore how these principles are practically implemented, bringing to life the transformative power of a mission-oriented approach in diverse organizational landscapes.

Questions about Defining Mission Parameters

Here are a few more interesting questions for you to consider and answer, as you contemplate how to use the insights about mission-oriented organizations presented in this book to your advantage:

1. **Mission Clarity:** How can an organization ensure that its mission is clearly understood by all members? What methods can be employed to prevent mission creep?

2. **Resource Allocation:** In what ways can an organization effectively balance its resource allocation to support its mission while maintaining operational efficiency?

3. **Risk Management:** What are some effective strategies for identifying and mitigating potential risks that could hinder a mission's progress?

4. **Stakeholder Involvement:** How can an organization identify and engage the key stakeholders relevant to its mission? What are the benefits and challenges of this engagement?

5. **Defining Success:** How can an organization establish clear, measurable criteria for success in relation to its mission? Can you provide an example of what this might look like?

6. **Flexibility and Adaptation:** How important is flexibility in mission parameters, and what are some best practices for adapting to changing circumstances without losing sight of the mission?

7. **Ethical and Legal Alignment:** Ponder for a while the importance of aligning a mission's parameters with legal requirements and ethical standards. How does this alignment benefit an organization?

8. **Feedback and Communication:** What are some effective ways to implement ongoing feedback and communication mechanisms within an organization, to continually refine and improve its execution of the mission?

9. **Purpose-Driven Actions:** Reflect on how purpose-driven actions can transform an organization. Can you think of an example where aligning decisions with a mission's core purpose led to significant and positive outcomes?

10. **Tesla Case Study:** What key lessons can be learned from Tesla's mission-driven approach, especially in the context of their response to the crisis in Puerto Rico?

11. **Values Alignment:** How does harmonizing an organization's actions with its values and mission contribute to building trust and authenticity among stakeholders?

12. **Impact-Centric Approach:** What are some challenges an organization might face when shifting to an impact-centric approach, and how can these be overcome?

13. **Long-Term Sustainability:** Discuss the importance of long-term sustainability in mission-oriented organizations. How can this be achieved while adapting to immediate changes and demands?

14. **Inspirational Culture:** What are the key elements that contribute to creating an inspirational culture in a mission-oriented organization? How does this culture impact employee engagement and productivity?

15. **Personal Reflection:** How can the principles discussed in this chapter be applied to your personal or professional life? Are there aspects of your current approach that could be aligned more closely with these principles?

As you can see, there is a lot to think about. But this reflection stage is an essential aspect of the Optimize the Moment methodology, which promises as much transformation as you desire and can handle, if you're ready to apply it within your organization.

Intelligence Gathering

Intelligence gathering, in the context of mission-oriented organizations, refers to the systematic process of collecting, analyzing, and interpreting information and data relevant to an organization's mission and objectives. It plays a crucial role in helping organizations make informed decisions, adapt to changing circumstances, and maximize their impact.

The Systematic Process of Intelligence Gathering

Intelligence gathering within mission-oriented organizations is not a haphazard or ad hoc activity. Instead, it is a systematic and deliberate process, one that involves several interconnected stages that ensure the collected information is accurate, relevant, and actionable.

The process begins with a clear identification of the specific information needs that are related to an organization's mission and objectives. What knowledge is essential for advancing the mission, in other words. This step sets the foundation for subsequent data collection efforts.

Data collection is the active gathering of information from various sources. These sources can deliver a wide range of information, harvested from market data, surveys, customer feedback, industry reports, academic research, and internal organizational data. Each source contributes to a more comprehensive understanding of the mission context.

Once data are collected, it must undergo rigorous analysis. This stage involves the systematic examination of data to identify patterns, trends, correlations, and insights. Data analysis transforms raw information into valuable knowledge that informs and improves decision-making.

Interpretation is the process of assigning meaning to the analyzed data. This step goes beyond the numbers and statistics to provide a contextual understanding of what the data signifies for the organization's mission. Interpretation helps decision-makers grasp the implications of the information, which is why it must be done rigorously and logically.

Ensuring data accuracy and reliability is critical. Mission-oriented organizations implement validation and quality assurance processes to verify the integrity of the information collected. This step minimizes the risk of relying on flawed or biased data.

Intelligence gathering operates as a feedback loop. As new information becomes available or circumstances change, the process repeats, allowing organizations to maintain a continuous flow of intelligence to inform their strategies and actions.

How Intelligence Gathering Supports Informed Decision-Making

Intelligence gathering serves as a cornerstone for informed decision-making within mission-oriented organizations. Here's how it aids in the decision-making process:

By monitoring and analyzing relevant data, organizations can identify potential risks and challenges that may hinder mission fulfillment. This information enables proactive risk mitigation strategies to be put in place.

Intelligence informs resource allocation decisions. Organizations can allocate their resources—financial, human, and technological—more effectively when they have a clear understanding of where the greatest impact can be achieved.

The insights gleaned through intelligence gathering contribute to the development of plans. Organizations can chart a course for the future that is informed by data and aligned with their mission and objectives.

Intelligence helps organizations identify opportunities that will dovetail with their mission. Whether it's entering new markets, forming strategic partnerships, or launching innovative initiatives, intelligence enables proactive decision-making to seize these opportunities.

By regularly assessing the outcomes of their actions in light of the collected data, organizations can gauge their progress toward mission objectives. This information enables them to adapt and refine strategies as needed.

Case Study: The Zara Model

Zara, a prominent player in the global fashion industry, is known for its fast fashion business model.

The company was founded in 1975 in La Coruña, Spain, by Amancio Ortega and Rosalía Mera. Ortega, who started his career in the clothing industry as a teenager, opened the first Zara store with Mera, his then-wife. The store was initially named Zorba, inspired by the movie Zorba the Greek, but was later renamed Zara due to a conflict with a nearby bar bearing the same name.

The philosophy behind Zara was to offer fashion-forward clothing at affordable prices. Ortega's approach was unique for the time, as he focused on understanding customer needs and rapidly responding to new fashion trends. He achieved this by significantly reducing the time between design, production, and delivery, a strategy that later became the cornerstone of Zara's business model.

In 1985, Ortega established Inditex (Industria de Diseño Textil, S.A.) as the holding company for Zara and other future brands. This move marked a significant expansion of the business. Zara continued to grow throughout the 1980s and 1990s, both in Spain and internationally. The first store outside Spain was opened in Portugal in 1988, and stores were then opened in the United States in 1989 and France in 1990.

Zara's rapid growth was driven by its unique business model, which integrated design, production, distribution, and retail all under one roof. This vertical integration allowed Zara to be highly responsive to changing fashion trends, often turning around new products in just weeks. Unlike traditional retailers that relied on seasonal collections, Zara's approach was to continuously introduce new items throughout the year, encouraging customers to visit their stores more frequently.

The use of advanced technology and sophisticated logistics systems also played a crucial role in Zara's success. The company used real-time data to track consumer preferences and quickly adapt its offerings. This focus on customer feedback and agile supply chain management enabled Zara to minimize overproduction and markdowns, making the brand both economically and environmentally more efficient than many of its competitors.

In the 21st century, Zara and Inditex continued to expand globally, opening stores in key markets and embracing e-commerce. Zara's ability to quickly produce and distribute fashionable items at an affordable price, its innovative use of technology, and its keen sensitivity to consumer trends have made it a leader in the fast fashion industry.

Zara's success is a testament to the importance of intelligence gathering. Their unique approach relies heavily on fast and efficient data collection from stores to understand consumer preferences in real time. Collected data is quickly communicated to their design and production teams, enabling them to adapt to changing market demands swiftly. The result is customer-centric product development, which is supported by regular analysis of market trends that allows Zara to stay ahead of the curve on fashion trends, ensuring they meet consumer demands effectively.

Adaptation to Changing Circumstances

Mission-oriented organizations operate in dynamic environments where external factors, such as market dynamics, social trends, and technological advancements, constantly evolve. Intelligence gathering equips these organizations with the flexibility needed to adapt to fluctuating circumstances, in the following ways:

Intelligence can serve as an early warning system, alerting organizations to emerging trends or potential disruptions. This foresight allows for timely responses and proactive adjustments in strategies.

Mission-oriented organizations engage in scenario planning, which involves considering various hypothetical scenarios and their potential impact on the mission. This anticipatory approach helps organizations prepare for multiple future possibilities.

Intelligence gathering results in valuable feedback that supports continuous improvement. Organizations can use the insights gained to refine their approaches, innovate, and remain responsive to evolving challenges and opportunities.

In mission-oriented organizations, intelligence gathering is a deliberate, systematic process that empowers these organizations to make informed decisions, navigate complex environments, and boost their impact. It is not merely about data collection, but also about transforming data into actionable intelligence that guides planning, supports informed decision-making, and ensures adaptability in pursuit of their mission and specific objectives.

Diverse Information Sources for Intelligence Gathering

Mission-oriented organizations recognize the importance of casting a wide net when gathering information. They draw insights from diverse sources, to construct a comprehensive and holistic view of the landscape in which they operate.

Here's a summary of how it works:

Market research is a foundational source of intelligence. It involves the systematic study of the market in which the organization operates. This includes analyzing market size, trends, customer behaviors, competitors, and emerging opportunities or threats. Market research helps organizations understand the dynamics of their industry and how that impacts their target audience.

Mission-oriented organizations actively seek feedback from their stakeholders. This includes customers, employees, partners, suppliers, and communities affected by their work. Stakeholder feedback provides valuable insights into their needs, expectations, concerns, and perceptions of the organization's impact.

Keeping abreast of industry trends and benchmarks is crucial for staying competitive and relevant. Organizations monitor industry publications, read many reports, and stay up to date on key performance indicators (KPIs) to assess how they compare with industry standards. These efforts help them identify areas for improvement.

Leveraging academic studies and research adds a layer of depth to intelligence gathering. Organizations tap into the wealth of knowledge produced by academic institutions, think tanks, and research organizations. Academic research provides evidence-based insights into various aspects of their mission, which makes it indispensable.

Government reports and regulations often contain valuable information for mission-oriented organizations, especially in areas relating to policy changes, compliance requirements, and potential government funding opportunities. Monitoring government sources helps organizations stay aware of relevant regulations, so they're prepared to seize government-related opportunities when they arise.

Data analytics plays a pivotal role in intelligence gathering. Organizations collect and analyze data from various digital sources, staying current on website analytics, social media engagement, customer databases, and online surveys. Data analytics provides real-time insights into customer behavior and preferences.

Understanding the strategies and activities of competitors is essential. Competitive intelligence involves monitoring and analyzing the actions, strengths, weaknesses, and innovations of rival organizations. This knowledge helps mission-oriented organizations differentiate themselves and innovate more effectively.

Mission-oriented organizations will regularly assess the social and environmental impact of their actions. They gather information on the outcomes and consequences of their initiatives to ensure alignment with their mission's social and/or environmental goals.

Research and partnerships with academic institutions, other organizations, and experts in the field provide access to specialized knowledge and data. These collaborations expand the organization's information network.

Staying informed about news and media coverage related to their mission area is vital. It helps organizations track public sentiment, identify emerging issues, and respond to developments that may affect their capacity to implement their vision.

Engaging with the communities they serve provides mission-oriented organizations with insights from the grassroots level. Community engagement can uncover unique challenges, identify special opportunities, and gain critical information about cultural factors that will impact their work.

Internal feedback mechanisms within the organization, such as employee surveys and performance evaluations, provide insights into organizational dynamics and employee satisfaction, while helping to uncover areas for improvement.

By harnessing these diverse information sources, mission-oriented organizations ensure that their intelligence-gathering process is robust, well-rounded, and capable of capturing the multifaceted aspects of their mission and the operating environment. This comprehensive approach enhances their ability to make informed decisions, adapt to change, and maximize their positive impact.

Data Collection and Analysis in Mission-Oriented Organizations

Data collection and analysis are fundamental components of intelligence gathering for mission-oriented organizations. This systematic process involves gathering relevant information and transforming it into actionable insights.

Here's an in-depth exploration of these two essential steps:

Data Collection

Surveys are a commonly employed data collection method. Organizations design surveys to gather structured data from respondents. Surveys can be administered in various formats, including online questionnaires, phone interviews, or in-person interviews. They help organizations collect quantifiable data on a wide range of topics, such as customer preferences, employee satisfaction, and community needs.

Interviews involve one-on-one or group conversations with individuals who possess valuable insights or expertise. These interviews can be structured or unstructured, allowing for in-depth exploration of specific topics. Interviews are particularly useful for capturing qualitative data and personal perspectives.

Data mining leverages technology to extract patterns, identify trends, and harvest information from large datasets. Organizations use data mining algorithms to discover hidden insights within their data, which can help inform decision-making. This method is especially valuable for organizations dealing with extensive data sets, such as those in healthcare or finance.

Social media platforms are a rich source of real-time data. Organizations monitor social media conversations, mentions, and sentiment to gauge public opinion, track trends, and assess their brand's online presence.

This method is crucial for organizations engaged in public advocacy or awareness campaigns.

Observational data is collected through direct observation of events, behaviors, or processes. Mission-oriented organizations may deploy observers to gather data on the ground; for example, they may be asked to assess community needs or track environmental changes. Observational data adds depth to interpretations of real-world situations.

Secondary data sources include pre-existing facts and figures from external sources, such as government reports, academic studies, industry publications, and market research. These sources provide valuable background information and context to complement primary data collection efforts.

Internal feedback mechanisms within the organization, such as employee feedback surveys or customer feedback forms, offer insights into organizational performance and help identify areas for improvement. This feedback is a valuable source of data for mission-oriented organizations.

Data Analysis

Raw data often requires cleaning and preprocessing to remove errors, outliers, and inconsistencies. This step ensures that the data used for analysis is accurate and reliable.

A good place to begin is with a clear objective that will illuminate what you aim to achieve with your data analysis. This will help you narrow your focus, so you're only analyzing data that relates directly to your goal and not wasting time looking at less relevant information. There are many AI tools available now that can help you sort the data properly.

Next, you may want to concentrate on analyzing a few key metrics, the landmarks that really define your journey. These are the aspects of your data that speak most clearly to your objectives.

As you interpret the data, you can remain focused on your final destination. How do these insights relate to your organization's goals and strategies, you can ask yourself. When you create reports, you can use visuals to highlight your most important discoveries, adding clarity to your analysis.

The good news is, each time you complete an analysis it will be a learning experience, an opportunity to refine your path and explore new routes. By treating data analysis as an ongoing journey of discovery, your organization can engage with data in a way that is manageable, enlightening, and fully aligned with your goals, all without feeling overwhelmed by the vastness of the information you had to study.

One key methodology that can prove highly useful, Exploratory Data Analysis (EDA), involves the visual exploration of data to identify patterns and relationships. Data visualization techniques, such as charts and graphs, help analysts gain initial insights into the information's structure and potential trends.

By visually exploring data through such techniques, it is possible to spot patterns that are crucial for preparing for and recognizing the big Moments that define the mission. This is vital for seeing the big picture.

What should be avoided is too much absorption in too much data. In my experience, it is better to focus on the key insights that have relevance to the mission, without drowning in a sea of information that has little or no importance. Every organization has different needs and capacities for data analysis, so leaders in each will have to reflect on what represents the right kind of intelligence gathering (i.e., what information will help point team members in the right direction as the mission unfolds).

When an organization collects and analyzes data strategically, greater comprehension and illumination will be the result. It becomes easier to seize the day and fulfill the mission, since the most important Moments will be more recognizable.

EDA, in this context, is not just an analytical process. It is a mission-critical tool that empowers organizations to make informed decisions, adapt to changes, and ultimately advance the mission more effectively.

Going further, statistical analysis techniques, including descriptive statistics, inferential statistics, and regression analysis, allow organizations to quantify relationships within the data. This analysis helps identify statistically significant patterns and correlations.

For qualitative data collected through interviews or open-ended survey questions, qualitative methods like content analysis or thematic analysis can be most helpful. These methods help uncover themes, narratives, and insights that might otherwise remain hidden in the data streams.

Advanced analytics techniques, such as predictive modeling, machine learning, and data clustering, can uncover complex insights and make predictions based on the data. These techniques are especially useful for organizations seeking to anticipate future trends or outcomes.

Data analysis obviously involves interpretation, and this is where having a well-conceived and articulated mission can be highly useful. Analysts interpret the results of their analysis in the context of an organization's mission and objectives, as they seek to answer critical questions and draw actionable insights. Organizations must continuously collect and analyze data, incorporating new insights into their strategies and actions. The feedback loop ensures that intelligence remains up-to-date and relevant.

As we can see, data collection and analysis are essential components of intelligence gathering within mission-oriented organizations. By employing diverse data collection methods and rigorous analytical techniques, these organizations can extract meaningful insights that inform strategic decisions, drive impact, and ensure alignment with their mission and objectives. The ability to turn data into actionable knowledge helps mission-oriented organizations navigate complex challenges and contribute effectively to their chosen causes.

Market Research in Mission-Oriented Organizations

Market research is a foundational component of intelligence gathering for mission-oriented organizations. It involves a systematic and thorough examination of the market or environment in which the organization operates. Market research provides valuable insights into competitors, consumer behaviors, emerging trends, and potential opportunities and threats.

A primary feature of market research is a thorough assessment of competitor capabilities. This analysis delves into competitors' strengths, weaknesses, current market share, strategies, and innovations. Understanding the competitive landscape helps organizations differentiate themselves and develop strategic advantages.

At the consumer level, mission-oriented organizations strive to understand their customers' behaviors and preferences. Market research examines consumer demographics and buying patterns and peruses customer feedback. The knowledge gained from such activities informs product or service development, marketing strategies, and approaches to customer engagement.

Market research keeps organizations abreast of emerging trends and shifts in the market. Whether it's technological advancements, cultural changes, or industry innovations, staying informed about trends helps organizations adapt and seize opportunities proactively.

Mission-oriented organizations use market research to assess potential opportunities to enhance the performance of their missions. This can include identifying underserved segments of the market, spotting unmet needs, or pinpointing areas where the organization's impact can be maximized.

Equally important is the identification of potential threats or challenges. Market research helps organizations anticipate and mitigate threats that could hinder mission fulfillment. This proactive approach is a crucial aspect of risk management.

The insights gained from market research serve as a foundation for planning. Organizations use this information to formulate strategies that align with their mission and objectives. This research informs decisions about where to allocate resources, reveals which initiatives to prioritize, and shows decision-makers how to position the organization within the market.

Resource allocation is a critical aspect of mission-oriented organizations. Market research aids in optimizing the allocation of financial, human, and technological resources. By understanding market dynamics, organizations can allocate resources to initiatives that offer the greatest potential to produce positive results.

Market research informs decisions related to market positioning. Organizations can determine how to position themselves effectively to reach target audiences and differentiate themselves from competitors. This positioning will be consistent with the organization's mission and values.

Understanding one of the key dynamics that determines successful performance, mission-oriented organizations prioritize customer-centric approaches. Market research helps organizations tailor their products, services, and outreach efforts to meet the needs and expectations of their customers or beneficiaries. This customer-centricity enhances mission impact; in a sense you could even say it defines what mission impact really means.

In recognition of the fluidity of consumer demand, market research must be an ongoing process. It allows organizations to adapt to changing market dynamics, shifts in consumer preferences, and alterations of competitive landscapes. By continuously monitoring market developments, organizations remain agile and responsive.

Market research often includes key performance indicators (KPIs) that measure the impact of organizational initiatives in the marketplace. This data-driven approach helps organizations assess the effectiveness of their mission-aligned strategies.

In short, market research is a vital tool for mission-oriented organizations. It provides a comprehensive understanding of the market, consumer behaviors, and external factors that impact mission fulfillment. By leveraging market research insights, these organizations can make informed decisions, allocate resources strategically, and stay in sync with a dynamic landscape to create meaningful and lasting impact that furthers their mission and its objectives.

Stakeholder Engagement in Mission-Oriented Organizations

Stakeholder engagement is a fundamental and ongoing process within mission-oriented organizations. It means actively involving various stakeholders, including employees, customers, partners, communities, and other relevant parties, in the organization's activities and decision-making.

Here's a detailed look at the characteristics and functions of stakeholder engagement:

Mission-oriented organizations recognize the value of diverse perspectives. Engaging with stakeholders allows the organization to tap into a wide range of insights, experiences, and viewpoints. This diversity enriches the organization's understanding of the complex issues that can impact its mission.

Stakeholder engagement makes it possible to identify and prioritize the needs of various stakeholder groups. It provides a platform for stakeholders to express their concerns, aspirations, and expectations as they relate to the organization's mission. This information guides the organization in tailoring its initiatives to meet these needs effectively.

Engaging with customers is crucial for mission-oriented organizations. It allows them to gather feedback on their products, services, and customer experiences. This customer-centric approach ensures that the organization's offerings precisely match the preferences and requirements of its customer base.

Meanwhile, engaging with employees fosters a culture of transparency and inclusivity. It enables organizations to assess employee satisfaction, gather ideas for improvement, and address workplace concerns quickly. Engaged and satisfied employees are more likely to be fully onboard with the organization's mission and contribute positively to its objectives.

For organizations with community-focused missions, engaging with local communities is essential. It builds trust, establishes partnerships, and ensures that community voices are heard and respected. Community engagement helps organizations tailor their initiatives to address specific community needs.

Mission-oriented organizations often collaborate with partners, whether they are other nonprofits, government agencies, or private sector entities. Stakeholder engagement facilitates the identification of potential collaborators, which can enliven missions by providing more resources to amplify impact.

In complex environments, conflicts may arise among stakeholders. Fortunately, effective stakeholder engagement provides a platform for open dialogue and conflict resolution. Addressing conflicts in a constructive manner helps maintain positive relationships and ensures continued mission alignment.

Stakeholder input informs strategic decision-making processes. Organizations use feedback and insights from stakeholders to make informed choices about mission initiatives, resource allocation, and long-term planning. In addition, stakeholder engagement often includes mechanisms for measuring the impact of the organization's work. Key performance indicators (KPIs) and feedback loops allow organizations to assess the effectiveness of their initiatives in meeting stakeholder expectations and mission goals.

Engaging with stakeholders fosters transparency and builds trust. When stakeholders feel heard and involved, they are more likely to trust the organization's intentions and support its mission. Trust is an indispensable asset for mission-oriented organizations.

Stakeholder engagement supports a culture of continuous improvement. Organizations use stakeholder feedback to refine their strategies, programs, and operations. This iterative approach ensures that the organization remains responsive to evolving needs and circumstances.

As a bonus, engaged stakeholders often become advocates and supporters of the organization's mission. They may actively promote the organization's work, contribute idea or resources, or participate in advocacy efforts, expanding the organization's reach and impact.

Stakeholder engagement is integral to intelligence gathering within mission-oriented organizations. It serves as a two-way communication channel that allows organizations to listen to the voices of their collaborators, and to those they serve. By actively engaging with stakeholders, these organizations gain valuable insights into everyone's needs, expectations, and concerns, enhancing their ability to fulfill their mission effectively and to make a positive impact in their chosen domains.

Risk Assessment in Mission-Oriented Organizations

Risk assessment is a critical aspect of intelligence gathering for mission-oriented organizations. It involves a systematic evaluation of potential hazards and challenges that could impact the organization's ability to fulfill its mission and objectives.

Here's an in-depth look at the significance of risk assessment:

Risk assessment begins with the identification of potential risks and challenges. Mission-oriented organizations analyze a wide range of factors, including those in the political, economic, social, technological, and environmental categories (this is commonly known as PESTEL analysis). Those who manage to navigate all the potential minefields successfully rely on consistent information gathering and objective and factual analysis to steer a sensible course. By identifying risks proactively, organizations can develop strategies to mitigate them.

Assessing risks helps organizations prepare for adverse scenarios while they build greater resilience. By understanding the potential challenges they may face, organizations can develop contingency plans, allocate resources for risk mitigation, and establish response protocols to minimize disruptions to their mission.

Among its more intriguing impacts, risk assessment informs resource allocation decisions. Organizations can allocate resources strategically by considering the likelihood and potential impact of different risks. This ensures that resources are directed toward mission-critical activities and the most impactful risk mitigation efforts.

Mission-oriented organizations often work in dynamic and unpredictable environments. Risk assessment supports adaptive planning, allowing organizations to adjust their strategies and initiatives in response to changing circumstances or newly emerging risks.

Risk assessment plays a vital role in strategic decision-making. Organizations use risk analysis to evaluate the feasibility and potential success of mission initiatives. It helps leaders make informed choices about which projects to pursue and how to use their resources more effectively.

To stay one step ahead, mission-oriented organizations engage in scenario planning based on identified risks. They create different scenarios that represent potential challenges and assess their implications. This helps organizations prepare for a range of outcomes, training them to adapt their strategies accordingly.

Ensuring mission continuity is a top priority for these organizations. Risk assessment helps them maintain their mission focus even in the face of unexpected disruptions. It ensures that the organization can continue to work toward the fulfillment of its mission, despite the challenges that arise.

Organizations often communicate their risk assessment findings with stakeholders, including employees, donors, partners, and beneficiaries. Transparency about potential risks demonstrates responsible stewardship and fosters trust.

In some cases, risk assessment is tied to compliance with regulations or contractual agreements. Organizations must adhere to specific requirements and ensure that their risk management practices always align with legal and ethical standards.

Mission-oriented organizations rely on data and evidence-based decision-making. Risk assessment is never done seat-of-the-pants, as it produces data-driven insights that inform decisions related to risk management and mission planning. By understanding potential risks that could lead to mission drift, organizations can proactively take steps to prevent deviations from their chosen directives and core values.

Conducting a risk assessment is a proactive and integral component of intelligence gathering within mission-oriented organizations. It enables these organizations to anticipate, prepare for, and respond to potential challenges and disruptions, while maintaining their focus on fulfilling their mission and remaining a force for positive change.

Case Study: Apple is a Master of Innovation and Risk Mitigation

Apple was founded on April 1, 1976, by Steve Jobs, Steve Wozniak, and Ronald Wayne. In those early days, Apple was significantly different from the tech giant we know today.

Initially, Apple's focus was on personal computers. The first product, the Apple I, was a far cry from today's sleek devices. It was essentially a circuit board sold as a do-it-yourself kit for hobbyists. Steve Wozniak was the technical genius behind it, while Steve Jobs had the vision to market it.

In 1977, Apple launched the Apple II, which was a huge success. This was one of the first successful personal computers and it really put Apple on the map. It had a color display, which was a big deal at the time, and appealed to both businesses and consumers.

Fast forward to today, and Apple has evolved into a diversified technology powerhouse. Under the leadership of Tim Cook, the company has expanded far beyond personal computers. Apple now offers a wide range of products and services, including the iPhone, iPad, MacBooks, Apple Watch, and services like iCloud and Apple Music.

What's remarkable is how Apple has consistently been at the forefront of design and innovation. From the sleek design of its products to the introduction of the App Store, which revolutionized software distribution, Apple has continued to redefine the technology landscape.

Apple's approach to innovation and risk mitigation, particularly with the iPhone, demonstrates a strategic blend of bold creativity and prudent risk management. Before the iPhone, Apple was known for computers and the iPod. Venturing into the smartphone market, dominated by established players, was a bold but perilous move.

However, Apple meticulously researched consumer preferences and leveraged its strengths in user interface and design. The iPhone's launch was a calculated risk, underpinned by a deep understanding of market gaps and technological capabilities.

Apple's success with the iPhone wasn't just about introducing a new product; it was about redefining a category and setting a precedent for how technology could integrate into people's lives. This case exemplifies how aligning innovative products with strategic risk assessment can lead to market leadership and shape industry trends.

Competitive Analysis in Mission-Oriented Organizations

For mission-oriented organizations operating in competitive environments, competitive analysis is a vital aspect of intelligence gathering. It entails systematically monitoring and analyzing the activities, strategies, and performance of competitors, to gain the edge wherever possible.

Here's a look at what competitive analysis involves:

Competitive analysis is a straightforward process. It means identifying and profiling competitors within the organization's sector or industry. This means identifying both direct competitors offering similar services or products, and indirect competitors whose activities may somehow affect the fulfillment of an organization's mission.

By studying competitors carefully without bias or preconceived notions, mission-oriented organizations gain important insights into their strategies. This includes assessing how competitors position themselves in the market, their pricing strategies, their approaches to marketing and messaging, and their customer engagement tactics.

Competitive analysis helps organizations spot opportunities for differentiation and innovation, which may involve making changes that are actually quite subtle. By understanding what competitors offer and how they operate, down to the most minute detail, successful organizations will identify gaps in the market they are prepared to fill.

Mission-oriented organizations use competitive analysis to refine their market positioning. They assess how competitors are perceived by stakeholders, and strategically position themselves to stand out based on their mission, values, and impact.

Benchmarking against competitors allows organizations to assess their performance and impact. By comparing metrics such as market share, growth rates, and mission-related outcomes with those of competitors, organizations can set more meaningful performance targets and track their progress at meeting those goals.

Competitive analysis provides data and insights that inform decision-making processes. Organizations can make informed choices about resource allocation, strategic partnerships, and the prioritization of initiatives based on developments across the competitive landscape.

Mission-oriented organizations often need to adapt their strategies to evolving market dynamics. Competitive analysis helps organizations identify shifts in customer preferences, anticipate emerging trends, and evaluate disruptive technologies that may impact their ability to complete their mission. This knowledge supports more adaptive planning.

Understanding how competitors engage with stakeholders, including customers, donors and partners, provides organizations with ideas for enhancing their own stakeholder relationships and engagement strategies. Competitive analysis also helps organizations identify potential strategic partners or collaborators, making it possible to build new partnerships with individuals or organizations that are pursuing a similar mission.

Competitive analysis is an essential element of intelligence gathering within mission-oriented organizations. It empowers these organizations to navigate competitive environments effectively, identify opportunities for differentiation and innovation, and make data-driven decisions that support their mission and objectives. By staying informed about the competitive landscape, mission-oriented organizations can maximize their impact and identify problem areas more rapidly.

Nevertheless, in my experience it is important to tread somewhat lightly when assessing competitor strategies, policies, and performance. At times organizations can become too preoccupied with what their competitors are doing, to the detriment of their own performance. In the end everyone's mission is unique, and the paths your competitors are following will always include elements that don't apply to your organization.

Scenario Planning in Mission-Oriented Organizations

Scenario planning is a forward-looking and proactive intelligence activity. It entails the creation of hypothetical scenarios that explore potential future developments and assesses their potential impact on an organization's mission and objectives.

Mission-oriented organizations often operate in dynamic and uncertain environments. Scenario planning allows these organizations to anticipate and prepare for a range of possible futures. It acknowledges the inherent uncertainty in the world and helps organizations prepare for challenging contingencies.

Scenario planning means identifying key drivers or variables that could significantly influence the outcome of an organization's mission. These drivers may include political, economic, social, technological, and environmental factors. Understanding these variables helps organizations focus on what matters most, while also helping to inform more strategic decision-making.

Scenario planning supports risk mitigation efforts. By exploring various scenarios, organizations can identify potential risks and challenges that may arise in different futures. This knowledge enables them to develop risk mitigation strategies specific to each scenario.

Questions of resource allocation are critical for mission-oriented organizations, and playing out different scenarios can have a constructive impact on resource allocation decisions. The most likely scenarios will have the biggest impact on planning and resource use, and ensure that resources are not squandered on low-probability contingencies. Nevertheless, mission-oriented organizations must remain adaptable in the face of changing circumstances, and high-quality scenario planning literally prepares them for just about anything.

Another benefit of anticipating different scenarios is that they challenge organizations to think creatively and innovatively. Exploring hypothetical futures stimulates new ideas and approaches that can enhance the organization's mission impact.

Relatedly, scenario planning fosters better communication within an organization. It encourages teams to discuss and prepare for multiple futures. As a result, actors within an organization become better prepared to respond effectively to unexpected events.

Scenarios help ensure that an organization's strategies remain aligned with its mission and values across different possible futures. This consistency is crucial for maintaining mission focus and impact.

Because of its inclusive nature, scenario planning allows organizations to engage with stakeholders, donors, and partners in discussions about potential future challenges and opportunities. This strengthens collaboration and mutual understanding.

Scenarios are not static; they evolve over time. Organizations use scenario planning as part of their ongoing monitoring and evaluation processes, to ensure the relevance and accuracy of the scenarios they imagine so they can adjust their strategies accordingly.

Scenario planning encourages a culture of continuous learning. Organizations reflect on the outcomes of scenarios and use the insights gained to refine their strategies and decision-making processes.

For those determined to always stay one step ahead, scenario planning is a proactive and forward-looking intelligence activity that empowers mission-oriented organizations to navigate uncertainty, make informed decisions, and enhance their preparedness and resilience. By considering a range of possible futures and outcomes, these organizations can strategically allocate resources, adapt to changing circumstances, and maintain their commitment to fulfilling their mission and making a positive impact.

Technology and Tools in Intelligence Gathering

Intelligence gathering in mission-oriented organizations is significantly improved by the use of various technologies and tools. These tools empower organizations to collect, analyze, and manage information efficiently, facilitating informed decision-making and mission fulfillment.

Technology and its associated tools enable organizations to collect and manage vast amounts of data. Among the most helpful tools are data analytics software, which processes and extracts insights from data sources, and customer relationship management (CRM) systems that centralize information about stakeholders, donors, and beneficiaries.

Let's take a closer look at some of these tools and how they work:

Automation tools streamline data collection and analytical processes. For example, social listening platforms can automatically monitor online conversations to "hear" what people are saying about the organization and its mission. This is an example of automation enhancing efficiency and reducing the manual workload.

Meanwhile, visualization tools transform complex data into visually accessible formats, such as charts and graphs. These visuals help stakeholders, including decision-makers, understand and interpret data more easily, supporting data-driven decision-making.

Market research tools and survey platforms enable organizations to gather feedback from stakeholders, donors, and beneficiaries. These tools facilitate the design, distribution, and analysis of surveys, which are invaluable for organizations determined to gain greater insight into their stakeholders' needs and expectations.

An essential element of intelligence gathering for any 21st century business, social media monitoring tools track online conversations and identify trends that have relevance to an organization's mission.

They provide real-time insights into public sentiment, enabling the organization to respond promptly to emerging issues.

Competitive intelligence tools are also highly useful, as they help organizations monitor and analyze competitors' activities. These tools track market developments, competitor positioning, and key performance indicators, which aids in planning and the development of strategies for differentiation.

For organizations that handle sensitive information (which is most), certain tools play a crucial role in ensuring data security and privacy. Robust cybersecurity measures, encryption, and secure data storage are essential for protecting sensitive mission-related data.

Predictive analytics tools use historical data to forecast future trends and outcomes. These tools help organizations anticipate potential challenges and opportunities, enabling proactive decision-making and risk mitigation.

Collaboration tools, such as project management platforms and communication software, facilitate internal and external communication among team members, stakeholders, and partners. Effective communication at this level supports highly efficient intelligence sharing and coordination.

There are technologies that assist in resource allocation and budgeting processes as well. Financial management software helps organizations allocate funds strategically to mission-critical initiatives, based on the nature of the intelligence gathered.

Tools for measuring and evaluating impact, including impact assessment software and performance tracking dashboards, help organizations assess the effectiveness of mission initiatives. This lets them adjust strategies as needed, and quickly enough so that inefficiencies are minimized.

Technology can also support a culture of continuous learning and improvement. Organizational leaders use data analytics and insights to refine strategies, adapt to changing circumstances, and increase mission impact.

Technological tools are integral to intelligence gathering within mission-oriented organizations. They enable organizations to collect and process data and information more rapidly and effectively, which leads to better decision-making processes, wiser resource allocation, improved communication, and more frequent mission fulfillment. Performance is optimized as a result, and that performance promises to get even better as each new generation of techno-tools is introduced.

Ethical Considerations in Intelligence Gathering

Ethical considerations play a critical role in intelligence gathering for mission-oriented organizations. Ensuring that data collection methods and practices adhere to legal and ethical standards is essential for building trust with stakeholders, maintaining the organization's reputation, and upholding its commitment to its mission.

Respecting data privacy and obtaining consent are ethical imperatives. Organizations must ensure that they collect and handle personal data in compliance with relevant data protection laws and regulations. Obtaining informed consent from individuals when collecting their data demonstrates respect for privacy rights.

Ethical intelligence-gathering practices prioritize transparency and accountability. Organizations should explain their data collection methods and data usage policies to stakeholders, while adopting mechanisms of accountability that ensure data is used responsibly and for mission-aligned objectives exclusively.

Ethical considerations include minimizing harm to individuals or communities affected by an organization's data collecting practices. Organizations should assess the potential impact of data collection on stakeholders and take measures to mitigate any potential harm or negative consequences.

Data collection and analysis should avoid discrimination and bias. Ethical intelligence gathering includes efforts to eliminate biases in data collection, analysis, and decision-making, to ensure fairness and equity. Organizations should always base decisions on accurate and unbiased information, avoiding the manipulation or selective use of data to serve specific interests.

Cultural sensitivity is vital in intelligence gathering. Organizations must respect cultural norms and practices when collecting data from diverse populations, to avoid causing unintended offense or harm.

When gathering data from vulnerable populations, such as children, marginalized communities, or individuals in crisis, ethical considerations become even more critical. Special safeguards should be in place to protect the rights and well-being of these groups. Intelligence gathering practices should be consistent with an organization's mission and values, and therefore in harmony with its core principles.

Ethical intelligence practices include robust data security measures. Organizations must safeguard collected data from unauthorized access and breaches, to guarantee their stakeholders' interests are always protected. In the same vein, ethical intelligence gathering requires strict compliance with applicable laws and regulations. Organizations must stay informed about legal requirements related to data collection, storage, and use, to makes sure they remain in compliance.

When using data from third-party sources, ethical considerations include assessing the source's credibility, ensuring the data's accuracy, and respecting any contractual or ethical agreements related to data usage.

In cases of ethical violations or unintended harm, organizations should have mechanisms in place for remediation. They must be prepared to address complaints, conduct investigations, and take corrective actions in a timely manner.

Ethical considerations are fundamental in intelligence gathering within mission-oriented organizations. Adhering to ethical principles ensures that data collection methods are legal, respectful of privacy, and consistent with the highest standards of morality. Such practices build trust with stakeholders, protect the organization's reputation, and demonstrate a strong commitment to honest and ethical conduct.

Continuous Learning in Intelligence Gathering

Mission-oriented organizations prioritize ongoing learning and adaptation based on insights gained from intelligence activities. This agility enables them to respond promptly to changing circumstances, and to enhance their mission's impact.

Continuous learning informs adaptive strategies. Mission-oriented organizations recognize that the external environment is dynamic. They use the intelligence gathered from that environment to adjust their strategies, initiatives, and approaches as needed, to remain effective in achieving their mission goals.

Organizations use continuous learning to test and refine different scenarios. By evaluating the outcomes of hypothetical scenarios in comparison to actual events, they gain insights into the accuracy of their assessments and can fine-tune their scenario planning accordingly.

Continuous learning promotes data-driven decision-making. Organizations collect and analyze data to evaluate the impact of their mission-related activities. These insights guide decisions on resource allocation, programmatic adjustments, and strategic shifts.

Organizations maintain a feedback loop with stakeholders, including beneficiaries, donors, partners, and employees. Continuous learning involves soliciting feedback, listening to concerns, and integrating stakeholder perspectives into decision-making processes.

Continuous learning supports better performance evaluation. Organizations assess the effectiveness of their initiatives and programs using key performance indicators (KPIs) and impact metrics. Lessons learned from performance evaluations inform future actions.

Innovation and creativity are synonymous with continuous learning. Organizations encourage their staff to think creatively and propose fresh solutions based on gathered intelligence. This culture of innovation enhances the organization's capacity to make a significant impact.

Through continuous learning, organizations can more easily identify best practices. By analyzing successful initiatives and case studies, they can replicate effective approaches and avoid repeating mistakes in future mission-related endeavors.

Continuous learning helps organizations optimize resource allocation. They assess the return on investment of different activities, adjusting resource allocation based on what the intelligence reveals.

Ongoing learning enables organizations to anticipate and mitigate risks. By monitoring evolving risks and threats, organizations can develop proactive strategies to minimize potential disruptions.

In the face of unexpected crises or challenges, continuous learning enables organizations to respond effectively. Lessons learned from previous intelligence activities inform crisis response plans and strategies.

Continuous learning ensures organizations remain aware of changes in the external environment. This includes shifts in regulations, emerging trends, evolving stakeholder expectations, and developments in the organization's field of operation.

Organizations invest in capacity-building based on continuous learning. They identify areas where staff or teams may require additional training or resources to empower their efforts to fulfill the mission.

In summary, continuous learning is a fundamental component of intelligence gathering within mission-oriented organizations. It empowers these organizations to adapt, innovate, and make data-driven decisions, as well as maximize their impact in an ever-changing world. By maintaining a commitment to ongoing learning and improvement, mission-oriented organizations remain flexible and responsive to the needs of their beneficiaries and stakeholders.

Decision Support in Intelligence Gathering

Decision support is the ultimate goal of intelligence gathering for mission-oriented organizations. It involves leveraging the analyzed information and insights to provide leaders and teams with the necessary tools and knowledge to make informed, data-driven decisions.

Here is why decision support is such a vital aspect of intelligence gathering:

Decision support ensures that leaders and teams have access to the information and insights they need to make informed choices. It empowers decision-makers with a comprehensive understanding of the situation, risks, opportunities, and potential outcomes. Furthermore, decision support keeps decision-making processes aligned with the organization's fundamental objectives. It ensures that every decision made is consistent with the organization's core purpose, values, and commitment to its mission.

Mission-oriented organizations use decision support to inform their planning processes. It assists leaders tasked with identifying strategic priorities, allocating resources effectively, and setting clear goals for mission-related initiatives.

Decision support aids in resource allocation decisions. By providing insights into the impact and feasibility of different initiatives, it guides organizations as they assess how financial, human, and other resources can be used most strategically.

Decision support means an enhanced ability to develop strong risk assessment and mitigation strategies. Organizations can proactively identify and address potential risks, reducing the likelihood of mission disruptions or negative impacts.

Decision support often involves more precise scenario analysis. Organizations explore different scenarios and their implications for mission outcomes, which helps leaders make decisions that account for various possible futures.

Decision support helps develop more relevant and useful performance evaluation criteria. It allows organizations to assess the effectiveness of mission-related activities, programs, and initiatives, enabling data-driven adjustments and improvements.

Decision support means more support for stakeholder perspectives. It incorporates feedback from beneficiaries, donors, partners, and employees into decision-making processes, ensuring that decisions are consistent with stakeholder needs and expectations.

Decision support enables real-time responses to emerging challenges or opportunities. Organizations can make quick but thoroughly informed decisions based on up-to-date intelligence, reducing response time and maximizing impact.

Decision support reinforces an organization's commitment to building a data-driven culture. It encourages a reliance on evidence and analytics rather than intuition alone, leading to more effective and accountable decision-making.

Decision support promotes accountability and transparency. Organizations can trace their decisions back to the data and insights that informed them, so that stakeholders and the public can understand why they did what they did.

Decision support encourages a culture of continuous improvement. Organizations can learn from the outcomes of decisions, refine their approaches, and make iterative improvements to achieve their mission more effectively.

Decision support is the central objective of intelligence gathering in mission-oriented organizations. It empowers leaders and teams to make informed, mission-consistent decisions that increase organizational effectiveness and efficiency. By leveraging intelligence and data, these organizations enhance their capacity to create positive change, fulfill their mission-driven goals, and adapt to the evolving challenges and opportunities that constantly alter their operating environment.

Questions about Intelligence Gathering

In this chapter on intelligence gathering in mission-oriented organizations, we emphasized the critical role of systematic data collection, analysis, and interpretation in driving informed decisions and adaptive strategies. This process, essential for navigating dynamic environments, encompasses various methods ranging from market research to stakeholder engagement and risk assessment.

As we transition to the next chapter on Objective Analysis, the focus shifts to integrating the insights learned from intelligence gathering into practical, mission-aligned actions, ensuring organizations remain responsive, impactful, and always respectful of their own core values in an ever-evolving landscape.

Before moving on, here are some more questions for you to ponder, as you consider how your current intelligence gathering capacities might be improved:

1. What is the primary purpose of intelligence gathering in mission-oriented organizations?

2. How does intelligence gathering support informed decision-making in these organizations?

3. How would you describe the systematic process involved in intelligence gathering?

4. Why is adaptability to changing circumstances important in intelligence gathering?

5. What is the significance of diverse information sources in this process?

6. What is the role of data collection and analysis in intelligence gathering?

7. How does market research contribute to intelligence gathering in mission-oriented organizations?

8. Why is stakeholder engagement in the intelligence gathering process so vital?

9. How is risk assessment conducted in mission-oriented organizations?

10. What is the role of technology and technological tools in enhancing intelligence gathering efforts?

Objective Analysis

Events on the world stage can explode into reality—or literally explode reality—without notice. On a volatile planet, every decision can potentially determine the future of an organization. As such, understanding the essence of objective analysis is more than just a strategic move; it's a survival skill. But what does objective analysis truly mean, especially when viewed through the lens of optimizing the moment?

Objective analysis, in its purest form, is the art of dissecting information with an unclouded lens, free from personal biases and preconceived notions. It's about stepping back from the heat of the moment and viewing the facts as they truly are, not as we wish them to be. In the high-stakes scenarios I've encountered, from conflict zones to boardrooms, the clarity provided by objective analysis has often been the beacon guiding us through a thick fog of complexities.

At its core, objective analysis involves a systematic examination of the data at hand. It requires asking the hard questions: What are the facts? Where do they lead? What are they telling us, devoid of any emotional or subjective overlay? In the essence of The Moment, objective analysis represents a critical juncture, as it is the point where decisions shift from reactive to proactive, from gut-driven to logical with clearly defined parameters.

But there's a catch—and it's a significant one in the context of today's fast-paced, information-overloaded world. The process of objective analysis demands discipline. It requires us to detach from the immediacy of The Moment and the emotional responses it may invoke.

This doesn't mean being impassive. It's about being smartly dispassionate. In high-pressure situations, where decisions can have far-reaching implications, such detachment is not just beneficial; it is imperative.

Objective analysis also involves looking at the data from multiple angles. It's like viewing a diamond, with each facet providing a different reflection or a different perspective. You rotate this gem of information, gleaning insights from each viewpoint, understanding that the whole picture is far more than the sum of its parts. This approach is especially vital in The Moment, where every decision can be a game-changer.

In my experience, the key to mastering the art of objective analysis lies in three fundamental principles that I will explain soon in more detail:

1. You should let the data lead the way. Emotions have their place, but when analyzing objectively, facts should be your foundation.

2. You should take a range of viewpoints into account in the analysis. Diversity here isn't just a buzzword; it's a critical tool that sharpens your understanding.

3. The world changes rapidly, and so does information. So, you should reassess and realign your analysis to stay in touch with and on top of an evolving landscape.

Evidence over Emotion in Objective Analysis

In the dynamic crucible of decision-making, where The Moment can be as fleeting as it is impactful, the principle of evidence over emotion stands as a bulwark against the storm of subjectivity.

This observation isn't meant to undermine the value of intuition or emotional intelligence, both of which have their rightful place in leadership. Rather, it's about prioritizing hard evidence as the cornerstone of objective analysis.

In the many high-stakes environments I've navigated, from geopolitical negotiations to corporate boardrooms, emotions often run high. Fear, excitement, passion, and urgency – these feelings are part and parcel of making decisions in The Moment. However, when it comes to objective analysis, we must pivot from these emotions to focus on evidence—cold, hard, unvarnished facts.

Why Evidence Over Emotion?

In complex scenarios, emotions can cloud judgment, leading to decisions that feel right but aren't necessarily smart. Evidence provides a clear path through the complexity, offering a solid foundation upon which to build your strategies.

Decisions based on solid evidence can be easily justified and defended. This is crucial in organizational settings where accountability is paramount. When you base your decisions on facts, you provide a transparent rationale that can withstand scrutiny.

Emotions can fluctuate, but facts remain constant. By prioritizing evidence, you ensure a level of consistency in your decision-making process. This consistency is key to maintaining trust and credibility, especially in leadership roles.

Clarity in Complexity: The Bedrock of Objective Analysis

For governments, business owners, and the CEOs and their consultants who must navigate the labyrinth of modern decision-making, where complexity is the rule rather than the exception, the quest for clarity becomes essential. This is especially true in the moments that matter—in other words, in The Moment.

When faced with intricate challenges, the temptation is to rely on gut instincts or hunches. But true leadership requires more. It demands a commitment to clarity, which is only achievable through an unwavering dedication to choosing evidence over emotion, every time.

The Essence of Clarity in Complexity

We're continually bombarded with an overwhelming amount of data. In the scenarios that we face, emotions can often lead to selective perception, or seeing only what we want to see.

Objective analysis, grounded in evidence, cuts through this noise, providing a clear, unbiased path. The concept means identifying relevant data amidst the chaos and using it to illuminate the way forward.

In every complex situation, there are signals, or key pieces of information that are crucial to understanding the whole picture. There's also noise—distracting, irrelevant data that can lead us astray. Distinguishing between these requires a disciplined approach that values hard evidence over emotional reactions.

Complex situations are often not what they seem on the surface. There are undercurrents or hidden factors that can significantly impact outcomes. Objective analysis helps identify these undercurrents, providing a deeper understanding of the situation. This deeper understanding is critical for making decisions that are not just reactive, but proactive and strategic.

Accountability and Justification in the Face of Complexity

As it relates to critical decision-making, particularly in those pivotal moments I refer to as The Moment, the ability to account for and justify one's decisions is not just a professional obligation, but a cornerstone of effective leadership. This is where the principle of evidence over emotion truly proves its worth, serving as both a shield and a compass, guiding leaders through the tumultuous seas of complex decision-making.

The Imperative of Accountability and Justification

The hallmark of great leadership is the ability to make decisions transparently. When decisions are based on solid evidence, leaders can clearly articulate the "why" behind their actions. This transparency is critical in building trust among teams, stakeholders, and the broader community.

In the heat of The Moment, where quick decisions are often required, the rationale behind these decisions can sometimes be lost. However, when such decisions are grounded in evidence, it becomes easier to rationalize them, even in retrospect, as every step taken can be accounted for and justified.

Given the high-profile nature of the business environment, decisions can come under intense public and private scrutiny. Evidence-based decisions stand up better to such scrutiny, as they are built on a foundation of facts and data rather than conjecture or impulse.

Strategies for Ensuring Accountability and Justification

One practical step for ensuring accountability is to document the evidence and thought processes responsible for every major decision. This practice not provides a future reference for understanding, but also serves as a valuable resource for learning and growth within the organization.

It takes effort, but it is wise to foster a culture where team members are encouraged to base their suggestions and decisions on evidence. An evidence-based culture promotes accountability, and also drives a more analytical and thoughtful approach to problem-solving.

One way to do it is to implement a system of regular reviews where decisions are revisited and reanalyzed. This process should not be about pointing fingers, but about understanding the effectiveness of decisions and learning from them. It helps in reinforcing the importance of basing decisions on evidence and being able to justify them.

For the sake of transparency, you should keep stakeholders informed about decision-making processes and the evidence that supports them. This level of engagement and transparency reinforces accountability and builds confidence among those who are impacted by these decisions.

The principles of accountability and justification serve as vital components of objective analysis. They reinforce the need for decisions to be made not in the shadow of emotions but in the light of evidence.

In The Moment, when the pressure is on and the stakes are high, this approach provides both a safety net and a clear path forward, ensuring that decisions are effective but also defensible in the long run.

Transparent Decision Making: Essential for Trust and Effectiveness

Throughout my career, I've learned that transparent decision making is not just a good practice; it is fundamental to building and maintaining trust, ensuring accountability, and fostering an inclusive team environment. In The Moment, where decisions can have far-reaching and sometimes immediate implications, transparency in decision-making becomes critical. It aligns with the evidence-over-emotion philosophy, ensuring decisions are made with clarity and fairness and are understandable to all involved.

The Importance of Transparent Decision Making

Transparency in decision-making builds trust within the team. When team members understand how and why decisions are made, they are more likely to trust their leaders and believe in the decision-making process. Understanding the rationale behind decisions can enhance team members' commitment to the chosen course of action. They are more likely to be invested in the outcomes when they feel part of the decision-making process.

A transparent approach encourages open communication within the team. It invites feedback and discussion, which can lead to better, more informed decisions. Transparent decision-making helps in avoiding misunderstandings and potential conflicts. When decisions are made and communicated clearly, it leaves little room for misinterpretation or speculation.

Transparency in how decisions are made promotes accountability both at the leadership level and within the team. It holds everyone accountable for their actions and decisions, leaving no one feeling as if they've been treated unfairly or unjustly.

Implementing Transparent Decision Making

Based on how some of the organizations and companies I've worked for have handled questions of transparency, I can offer the following suggestions for how to make the decision-making process in your workplace or organization more open and transparent:

- Everyone should try to be as clear about the reasons for your decisions as possible. They can explain their reasoning, the information considered, and the expected outcomes.

- It can be good policy to involve team members in the decision-making process wherever possible. This inclusion can range from gathering input to making collaborative decisions.

- You'll win favor by establishing mechanisms for feedback and discussion about decisions. This could include regular meetings, open forums, or anonymous suggestion systems.

- You can try keeping detailed records of how decisions are made and share this information with the team. This practice will show everyone that your organization takes transparency seriously.

- When conflicts or concerns arise, you should try to address them right away to clear the air. You can discuss the issues raised and explain how they were considered in the decision-making process.

- If your leadership is a model of transparent decision-making, you'll win everyone's respect. Your thoughtful actions will set the tone for the rest of the team and the organization.

In The Moment, transparent decision-making ensures that every decision is not only made with a clear understanding of the situation, but is also communicated and understood by all stakeholders involved. This approach fosters a team culture that values openness, accountability, and mutual respect. These are essential qualities for any team facing challenging and dynamic environments.

Making Rational Choices in The Moment

The ability to make rational choices in The Moment is a critical skill that I've noticed and admired throughout my career. It involves a disciplined approach to decision-making, where choices are made based on sound reasoning, facts, and a thorough analysis of the situation, rather than on impulse, emotion, or unverified assumptions.

The Essence of Rational Choice

Being rational means setting aside personal feelings or biases and focusing on logical reasoning and facts. While emotions are a natural part of the human experience, allowing them to dominate decision-making can lead to choices that are not in the best interests of the mission or the team.

To make sure you're grounded in rationality, you can focus on data, research, and factual information to make decisions. This approach keeps your choices grounded in reality and is more likely to lead to successful outcomes.

Of course, you should also try to grasp the full context of the situation before making a decision. This means considering the potential impact of the decision on various stakeholders, and also evaluating that decision's long-term implications.

Thoroughness here requires critical thinking to evaluate different options, potential risks, and benefits. Assumptions should be questioned, information should be analyzed from various angles, and creative thinking should be encouraged to identify the best possible solution.

In The Moment, decisions often need to be made quickly. However, speed should not compromise the thoroughness of the decision-making process. Decisions should be rapid but carefully considered, which is key in dynamic environments.

Logic Over Emotion in Decision-Making: A Key to Strategic Clarity

In my experience, prioritizing logic over emotion will point you in the right direction when you must make a tough decision. While emotions are an intrinsic part of being human, allowing them to dominate decision-making can lead to choices that are less than optimal, which you will regret later. In contrast, a logic-driven approach offers clarity, consistency, and objectivity, key elements in making sound, strategic decisions.

The Rationale for Logic-Driven Decisions

Logic-based decisions rely on objective analysis of facts and data. This minimizes the risk of biases and errors that can arise from emotional responses. Logical decisions are more likely to be consistent since they are based on rational analysis rather than fluctuating emotional states.

Emotions are often tied to immediate feelings or reactions, whereas logic is aligned with long-term goals and strategies. Logical decision-making supports a forward-looking and strategic vision. Decisions made logically are also easier to explain and justify, which enhances the leader's credibility and the team's trust in their judgment.

Emotional decisions can sometimes lead to impulsive or risky choices. Logic provides a framework for assessing risks more accurately and making more calculated decisions.

Case Study in Logic over Emotion: Blockbuster vs. Netflix

The Blockbuster vs. Netflix case exemplifies adaptability in the face of industry evolution.

Initially, Blockbuster dominated the movie rental industry with its extensive network of physical stores. However, as internet accessibility improved, consumer preferences shifted toward online streaming.

Netflix, which started as a mail-order DVD rental service in 1997, recognized this shift early. They pivoted to online streaming in 2007, offering a vast library of films and TV shows made accessible via the internet. This move tapped into the growing desire for instant, convenient access to entertainment.

By contrast, Blockbuster was slow to respond to these market changes (not unlike Kodak as the culture moved from analog to digital cameras). Despite a late attempt to introduce an online service, Blockbuster couldn't match Netflix's offerings or adapt its business model effectively. Blockbuster's reliance on physical rentals became increasingly outdated, leading to a decline in customers and revenue.

Ultimately, Netflix's foresight and willingness to embrace new technology led to its rise as a streaming powerhouse. Blockbuster's failure to adapt led to bankruptcy in 2010. This case is a powerful lesson in the importance of agility and innovation in business strategy.

Balancing Logic and Emotion

While decisions should be logic-driven, understanding their emotional impact on stakeholders is important. This ensures empathy and consideration during the implementation stage.

Leaders should use emotional intelligence to understand and manage their own emotions and those of their team members, ensuring a harmonious and productive working environment.

Positive emotions can be powerful motivators. Thoughtful leaders can take advantage of this by framing logical decisions in a way that also appeals to the team's emotions.

Implementing a Logic-Driven Approach

You can demonstrate your commitment to logic over emotion by establishing clear, well-thought-out processes where decisions are made based on data and evidence. In doing so you'll be taking an important first step in encouraging the development of a culture where opinions backed by facts are always appreciated.

To make everyone a participant in the creation of this new culture, you can offer training to enhance critical thinking and analytical skills among team members. You can also implement a practice of regularly reviewing decisions to ensure they were based on sound logic and aligned with strategic objectives.

Demonstrating that your interest in building an evidence-over-emotion culture is for everyone's benefit, you should encourage all team members to provide feedback or raise concerns if they feel emotionally driven decisions have been made. This acts as an important check and balance mechanism that will ensure everyone remains on the right path.

Evidence-Based Decisions: The Bedrock of Strategic Implementation

It's imperative to consistently prioritize evidence-based decision-making. This approach ensures that every decision is grounded in factual, objective data, rather than conjecture or instinct. You'll be making informed choices that are defensible, transparent, and aligned with the mission's objectives.

Understanding Evidence-Based Decisions

At the heart of evidence-based decisions is data. This includes quantitative data like statistics and metrics, as well as qualitative data like case studies and expert opinions.

One key aspect is the minimization of personal biases. Decisions should be based on evidence, not personal preferences or assumptions, and your determination to root out bias should be relentless.

Staying grounded in evidence requires a thorough analysis of available information, considering all relevant factors and potential outcomes. Evidence-based decisions are transparent and can be easily explained and justified. This fosters accountability and trust within the team.

Implementing Evidence-Based Decision-Making

Based on my experience, there are a few principles to observe that can keep you entrenched in evidence-based decision-making:

- The data you collect should be high quality, relevant data from reliable sources. This could include market research, internal performance metrics, customer feedback, or industry reports.

- You should never be reluctant to critically evaluate the evidence. You can look for biases in the data, assess the reliability of sources, and consider the context of the information.

- It would be really smart to involve a diverse group of stakeholders in the decision-making process. You'll likely find that different perspectives can help in interpreting data more comprehensively.

- Since market trends and buying habits can shift on a dime, you should try to find the most up-to-data data to help you make decisions. As you've likely already noticed, what was true yesterday doesn't always hold up for today.

- While quantitative data provides the numbers, qualitative data offers context. Both are helpful, and you should try to collect both types of data to assist you in making well-rounded decisions.

- Your team members would probably appreciate some training on how to improve their data literacy. This will clear up any potential confusion by helping them learn to interpret and use data more effectively.

Evidence-Based Decision Making in Action

To deepen your experience in using evidence to make decisions, you should use the data you obtain to create various scenarios and forecast potential outcomes. This helps in anticipating future challenges and opportunities.

To gather good-quality evidence, you can implement systems to track and analyze performance data. You can use this data to make decisions about strategy, allocate resources, and find areas in need of improvement. You can also get more good information by establishing feedback systems that will allow you to gather insights from employees, customers, and other stakeholders. This is yet more evidence you can use to inform decisions.

Practical Steps to Ensure Rational Choices

When it comes to making rational decisions, everyone can use a little honing. Here's how you can make some improvements in this area, for yourself and your organization:

- You can strive to create a structured process for decision-making. This could include steps like identifying the problem, gathering information, considering alternatives, weighing pros and cons, and then making a decision.

- You should be eager to consult with team members or experts to gain different perspectives. This can help in identifying blind spots and enhancing the quality of the decision.

- You can work diligently to train yourself and your team in decision-making skills. To accomplish this, you can try exercises in critical thinking, scenario planning, and risk assessment.

- You can focus on balancing the necessity to make quick decisions with the need for accuracy. You might do this by having pre-set criteria or frameworks for decision-making already in place.

- After making a decision, you can conduct a post-decision analysis to understand its effectiveness. This helps in learning from each decision and improving future decision-making processes.

- While focusing on logic, you should also try to cultivate emotional intelligence, in yourself and in your staff and employees. This helps in understanding and managing one's emotions and the emotions of others, which is crucial in the decision-making process.

In The Moment, rational choices are those that are informed, logical, and effective, and perfect for steering the mission toward success. You can rely on evidence and reason as your guides, while also considering the human element and the broader context. This approach ensures decisions are not only strategic, but also realistic and responsible.

Defending Decisions Under Scrutiny: Ensuring Accountability and Confidence

I have learned the importance of not just making decisions, but also being able to defend them under scrutiny. This involves clearly articulating the reasoning, evidence, and considerations that led to a decision, which ideally you'll be able to do when faced with doubt, skepticism, or opposition. This aligns with the evidence over emotion philosophy, ensuring that decisions are made rationally and can be substantiated when questioned.

The Essence of Defending Decisions

Defending decisions under scrutiny promotes transparency. It shows that decisions were not made arbitrarily but were based on sound reasoning and data. Being able to justify decisions builds trust among team members, stakeholders, and the wider audience. It demonstrates that decision-makers are thoughtful, responsible, and accountable for their actions.

When leaders defend their decisions, it sets a precedent for a culture of accountability within the organization. It encourages others to also think critically and be prepared to justify their own decisions. The need to defend decisions ensures that they are made with greater care and consideration, knowing they will need to stand up to scrutiny.

The process of defending decisions often provides an opportunity for learning and improvement. It allows for reflection and can offer insights that refine future decision-making processes.

Strategies for the Defense of Decisions

To be able to defend decisions effectively, consider the following:

- You can keep thorough records of how decisions are made, including the data used, alternatives considered, and the rationale for the final choice.

- You can try to always communicate decisions clearly, along with their underlying rationale. This transparency is key in pre-empting misunderstandings and misinterpretations.

- You should strive to create an environment where constructive feedback is encouraged. This openness to scrutiny will keep everyone moving forward and improving.

- When defending decisions, this would be a great time to practice active listening. This will help you understand the concerns and questions of others, so you can address them directly in your defense.

- You'll likely want to stay informed about the latest developments related to the decision. Being well-prepared in this way will allow you to defend the decision more effectively if it is questioned in the future.

It's important to view scrutiny not as a threat, but as an opportunity to validate the veracity of the decision. You should embrace these challenges as a normal part of the decision-making process.

Defending decisions under scrutiny is about ensuring that decisions are not just made with the best available information and intention, but are also robust enough to withstand external examination. This process is key to maintaining credibility, trust, and confidence, both within and outside the organization.

Consistency in Decision Making: The Pillar of Objective Analysis

In the ever-changing landscapes of business and geopolitics, where The Moment can shift the trajectory of entire organizations or even nations, consistency in decision-making emerges as a critical anchor. The concept of evidence over emotion plays a pivotal role here, acting as the steady hand guiding decision-making across varied and often turbulent situations.

Throughout my career, I've learned the importance of understanding which levers can be controlled or used most effectively in decision-making. You have to be able to discern what's actionable and what lies beyond our power to influence.

Too often leaders mistakenly focus on factors they can't really manage. For example, while I was in Iraq, the focus was predominantly on security, which is largely out of the control of people in Parliaments. I realized that one way we could help was to encourage them to concentrate on actionable areas, such as infrastructure and public services.

Identifying and acting on controllable levers is essential for success and is a cornerstone of the suggestions I offer—based solely on my observations—in my book and with my clients. Recognizing and utilizing these levers is key to navigating complex situations, whether they involve restoring basis services in conflict areas or steering a company through market upheavals.

The Role of Consistency in Complex Environments

Consistency in decision making fosters an image of reliability and predictability in leadership. When stakeholders, employees, and peers know that your decisions are based on evidence and not whims, it builds a foundation of trust and credibility.

In the chaos of The Moment, a predictable framework for decision-making can be incredibly powerful. Consistency in how decisions are made, relying on facts and data, provides a clear pathway for action, even under the most unpredictable circumstances.

Consistent decision-making methodologies allow for solutions that are scalable across a multitude of scenarios. By applying a similar evidence-based approach, whether resolving a small internal matter or making a large-scale strategic decision, you ensure that your problem-solving strategies are adaptable and applicable on any level.

Cultivating Consistency in Decision-Making

Being consistent in decision-making procedures isn't always as easy as it sounds. We will inevitably slip up from time to time, failing to meet our highest standards in this regard.

Based on my observations, here are some tips that can help you make sure this doesn't happen:

- It's a good idea to develop and try to adhere to standardized processes for gathering and analyzing evidence, and for basing decisions on it. This doesn't mean all decisions are the same, but the process through which they are reached should be as consistent as you can make it.

- It's important to realize that consistency doesn't mean inflexibility. You can learn from each decision and adapt your approach to evidence gathering and analysis when that seems appropriate.

This iterative process ensures that your decision-making evolves in changing environments and when presented with new information.

- Consider always checking to make sure your decision-making aligns with the broader values and goals of the organization. Doing this will keep you focused on your organization's most important needs and prevent you from steering off course.

- To help your teams, you can provide them with frameworks and tools for evidence-based decision-making. This type of empowerment not only fosters consistency across the organization, but also encourages a culture of accountability and transparency.

- You can adopt the principle that consistency requires regular review and calibration. Working within this framework, you can set up mechanisms to periodically review decisions, the processes that led to them, and their outcomes. This review will ensure that your approach remains relevant and effective.

In the context of The Moment, where decisions often need to be made swiftly and under pressure, the principle of consistency in decision-making becomes even more critical. It is the steadying force that guides leaders through the storm of immediate challenges and into a future that is navigated with precision, foresight, and an unwavering commitment to favoring evidence over emotion.

Evidence over Emotion in Application

In essence, consistency means always choosing evidence over emotion when it comes time to make a critical decision. Here's some ideas for how to stay on the straight and narrow in that regard:

You should truly embrace a data-driven approach, making this an active and daily choice. In today's world, we have unprecedented access to information, and you can use this to your advantage. You can analyze trends, study reports, and gather statistics. You can then let these data points guide your understanding of the situation.

It is important to understand that emotions often lead us to make assumptions. If you spot an assumption in your reasoning you can challenge it, asking yourself, "Is this assumption based on a feeling or a fact?" This critical questioning is essential in separating what we believe to be true from what is actually true.

Sometimes, we are too close to a situation to view it objectively. In such cases, we can always benefit from seeking the counsel of those who can provide an unbiased perspective. This could be advisors, mentors, or even team members who aren't directly involved in the matter at hand.

Before finalizing a decision, it can be most informative to stress-test it against all possible scenarios and outcomes. How does it hold up under different conditions? Is your decision still sound when stripped of its emotional underpinnings? This practice is a powerful tool to guarantee that your decisions remain sound and sensible.

While it's true that emotions are an undeniable part of being human, they can sometimes lead us astray, especially in The Moment when a critical decision must be made. By championing evidence over emotion, we create a framework for making decisions that are rational, defendable, and aligned with our long-term objectives. This approach has been instrumental in my own career, which is why I recommend it as a guiding principle for anyone seeking to navigate the complex landscapes of today's world with clarity and conviction.

Embracing Diverse Perspectives: A Cornerstone of Decision-Making in The Moment

I have learned the indisputable value of embracing diverse perspectives. In The Moment, where decisions need to be both rapid and well-informed, seeking and integrating a variety of viewpoints is not just beneficial, it's imperative. This approach is critical in adhering to the principle of 'evidence over emotion,' as it ensures that decisions will be enriched by a wide range of insights and experiences.

The Power of Diverse Perspectives

Diverse perspectives bring different insights, experiences, and knowledge to the table. This variety sharpens the focus of the decision-making lens, allowing for a more comprehensive understanding of the situation at hand.

Homogeneity in thought and opinion can lead to echo chambers, where ideas are reinforced but not challenged. Diverse perspectives break this cycle, introducing fresh viewpoints and challenging preconceived notions.

A blend of diverse thoughts and experiences fosters creativity and innovation. It encourages outside the box thinking and leads to more inventive and effective solutions.

Strategies for Incorporating Diverse Perspectives

I've discovered that exposure to diverse perspectives and opinions can be a genuinely enlightening and enjoyable experience.

To appreciate how beneficial and even exhilarating this can be, you can try recruiting and working with team members who come from varied backgrounds and disciplines. This diversity should encompass not only demographic aspects, but also cognitive and experiential differences.

You may be doing so already, but if not, you may find it helpful to cultivate an environment where all opinions are valued and encouraged. You can create safe spaces where team members feel comfortable expressing their views without fear of judgment or reprisal.

To get the most out of the diversity of opinions around you, you might want to try developing your active listening skills even further. You can give full attention to different perspectives, considering them thoughtfully and engaging with them fully, to understand the rationale behind them.

Another great idea is to look beyond your organization for diverse perspectives. This could involve consulting with industry experts, community leaders, customers, or even competitors. This will help you challenge organizational and personal assumptions, which may be holding you back in subtle or surprising ways.

In today's interconnected world, considering global perspectives is crucial. Understanding how different cultures and societies might view a situation can provide invaluable insights.

In those moments where swift and effective decision-making is crucial, embracing diverse perspectives is not merely about ensuring representation; it's about making decisions that are more informed, balanced, and effective. This approach aligns with the principle of evidence over emotion by ensuring that our decisions are shaped by a comprehensive understanding of diverse viewpoints, rather than being constrained by a narrow focus.

Seeking External Inputs: Broadening Perspectives in The Moment

It's important to seek external inputs in The Moment—those pivotal instances where decision-making carries significant weight—because relying solely on internal resources and perspectives can be limiting. External inputs offer fresh insights, challenge internal biases, and broaden the scope of the decision-making process, aligning with the principle of evidence over emotion.

The Value of External Inputs

External inputs can introduce new ideas, viewpoints, and expertise that might not be available within the team or organization. This diversity of thought can be invaluable in challenging assumptions and sparking innovative solutions.

Consulting with external sources can either validate an organization's internal assumptions and decisions or call them into question, thereby providing a more objective assessment. External consultants, industry experts, and academic researchers can offer specialized knowledge and expertise that may not be present internally, particularly in areas that are rapidly evolving or highly specialized.

Strategies for Seeking External Inputs

So, what are some of the best strategies for obtaining useful external inputs? Here are a few suggestions that have produced good results for many businesses or organizations:

One obvious approach is to engage with thought leaders, industry experts, or academics who can provide insights based on their research, experience, and expertise in specific fields. This could be most enlightening, and you could undoubtedly have some fascinating dialogues with these individuals. You might be able to contact these people through industry forums, conferences, and workshops, where you can meet all types of interesting people while networking with peers and learning more about the latest emerging trends in your field.

Additionally, if you're intrigued by the idea of forming new relationships with talented or knowledgeable people, you can try to establish collaborations with external partners, suppliers, or other stakeholders who might offer a different perspective on the challenges and opportunities your organization faces.

Another way to get thought-provoking information is to utilize the services of market research and data analysis firms. Should you choose this option, their data could help you gain an understanding of market trends, customer preferences, and other external factors that could impact decision-making.

Your customers or end users might have a lot of interesting things to tell you, which is why you might consider implementing mechanisms to collect their feedback. This direct input can be particularly valuable in understanding market needs and learning more about people's responses to your products or services.

The practice of seeking external inputs is a strategic approach to ensure that decision-making is grounded in a comprehensive understanding of the landscape. No organization exists in a vacuum, and gaining fresh knowledge that illuminates the broader context—be it market dynamics, technological advancements, or global trends—can play a constructive role in shaping effective decision-making.

Regularly Challenging Assumptions: Becoming More Agile in The Moment

My experiences in dynamic and often unpredictable environments have taught me the importance of questioning the status quo. Regularly challenging assumptions is a valuable practice in these settings, where circumstances can change rapidly and sound decisions need to be made swiftly.

In many instances, both personal and professional, I've learned that assumptions can be either a guiding light or a deceptive mirage. In The Moment, where decisions hold immense power, challenging assumptions is not just a worthwhile practice, but a necessity for ensuring our actions are based on reality and not on potentially flawed preconceptions.

Why Challenging Assumptions is Essential

Assumptions, if left unchallenged, can lead to complacency. Regularly questioning these assumptions fosters a culture where continuous improvement and adaptation are expected.

In fast-paced or volatile environments, what was true yesterday may not make sense today. Challenging assumptions allows for quicker adaptation to new information, or to changes in circumstance.

By questioning the way things have always been done, new and innovative solutions can emerge. It breaks down mental barriers and opens up new possibilities for problem-solving.

Unexamined assumptions can hide potential risks. Regular scrutiny of these assumptions can reveal blind spots in strategies and plans, allowing for proactive risk management.

Business moves at warp speed, and regardless of how large or small the company is they need to be willing to pivot, sometimes with little or no advance notice. As such, complacency can be the biggest adversary to growth and innovation. To optimize the moment, organizations must actively guard against complacency by prizing and rewarding continuous improvement and adaptability.

There are several ways you can reshape your working environment to guarantee that assumptions are being questioned:

- You can try to create an environment where learning and skill development are continuous processes. Regular training, workshops, and exposure to new ideas may keep the team engaged and updated.

- It could be smart to encourage team members to regularly question existing processes. This practice helps identify areas for improvement, along with new opportunities.

- You could perhaps give awards for innovative ideas and successful implementation of those ideas. Recognition for creative solutions may motivate the team to think outside the box more often.

- You may want to implement a system of regular performance evaluations, not just to assess productivity but also to identify areas where complacency might be setting in.

- You should try to keep abreast of industry changes and competitor actions, which can serve as a catalyst for change within your organization.

- To prevent stagnation from setting in, you can encourage diversity as a method for ensuring fresh viewpoints are heard regularly.

By challenging assumptions, organizations can create a dynamic and forward-thinking environment that naturally prevents complacency and promotes continual growth and adaptation.

In The Moment, challenging assumptions is about ensuring that decisions are made based on a thorough and current understanding of the situation. It's a process that requires vigilance, curiosity, and a willingness to embrace change and uncertainty. This approach is crucial for operating in complex environments where adaptability and agility are keys to success.

This all leads nicely into being able to adapt to changing environments. This can start with an analysis of how rapidly evolving market trends and consumer behaviors demand flexibility in business strategies. Such an analysis will probably highlight the role of technology in driving change, and look more closely at how businesses can leverage these advancements to stay ahead of the curve.

As assumptions are questioned, it will add extra weight to your efforts to develop a workplace culture that embraces change, encourages innovation, and is willing to experiment and take calculated risks. In your interactions with staff and employees you can emphasize how failures and setbacks can be powerful learning opportunities, leading to the adoption of more robust and adaptable business practices in the end.

Case Study: Airbnb's Ability to Adapt During the Covid-19 Pandemic

Airbnb, which is primarily known for its home-sharing platform, faced an unprecedented challenge when the COVID-19 pandemic and subsequent lockdown struck. With global travel coming to a near halt, their traditional business model was severely impacted. Recognizing the need to adapt quickly, Airbnb launched "Online Experiences" in April 2020.

This initiative was a strategic pivot, allowing hosts to offer virtual experiences, such as cooking classes, art workshops, and historical tours, conducted over video platforms like Zoom. This move catered to the growing demand for virtual connection and entertainment during lockdowns. It not only provided a new revenue stream for Airbnb and its hosts, but also helped maintain customer engagement.

Online Experiences ranged from meditation with Buddhist monks in Japan to making pasta with Italian chefs. These sessions were designed to be interactive, giving participants a chance to learn new skills and virtually travel from the comfort of their homes. The program was a success, with thousands of experiences offered and booked by users from over 30 different countries within the first two months.

Airbnb's swift response to the pandemic through Online Experiences is a testament to its agility and innovative spirit, and its willingness to question assumptions about what made sense. It demonstrates how businesses can pivot and find opportunities in challenging situations, emphasizing the importance of being adaptable and responsive to change in today's dynamic business environment.

Here are a few other examples showing how companies pivoted beyond their initial mission, vision, and/or offerings in services and products to meet consumer demands, address sustainability, or take advantage of shifts in technology:

Spotify's Shift from Music Streaming to Podcasts: The company adapted wisely to market trends by expanding beyond their original mission to include podcast streaming, catering to the growing demand for diverse audio content.

Dyson's Expansion into Air Purifiers: A company known for vacuum cleaners expanded its mission to include air purifiers, capitalizing on its expertise in air manipulation technologies.

IBM's Transition to Cloud and AI Services: This bold action allowed a traditional hardware company to transform into a leader in cloud computing and AI, aligning its mission with evolving technological trends. And while AI is certainly controversial, it is poised to be transformative, impacting various sectors including healthcare, transportation, education, and industry.

PepsiCo's Acquisition of Healthy Snack Brands: The shift in consumer preference toward healthier options was noted by PepsiCo, stimulating a diversification of their portfolio to include nutritious snacks and beverages.

Unilever's Sustainable Living Plan: Unilever made the decision to integrate sustainability into their business model, illustrating a commitment to social and environmental responsibility while maintaining profitability.

On the Topic of Artificial Intelligence

We can expect advancements in AI to improve medical diagnostics, increase personalized learning, enable autonomous vehicles, and boost efficiency in manufacturing. AI will also play a significant role in data analysis and decision-making processes, potentially leading to more efficient and informed outcomes.

However, this future also brings challenges, like job displacement. It also raises ethical concerns, illustrating the need for robust AI governance to ensure equitable and safe implementation of AI technologies. Going forward, the focus will likely be on balancing innovation with societal and ethical considerations.

Optimizing the Moment: Challenging Assumptions and Adapting on the Fly

Each of the case studies mentioned above provides insights into how companies can evolve their mission and optimize their operations in response to changing market demands and societal expectations. Encouraging innovation means delving into strategies and practices that foster a culture of creativity and forward-thinking, which will prepare an organization for the most daunting challenges of the 21st century.

Here are just a few ways you can go about establishing this type of culture:

- You can strive to create a workplace where new ideas are welcomed and encouraged. This involves providing spaces for brainstorming and collaboration and encouraging team members to think outside the box.

- You can reward your employees by giving them the autonomy to experiment with new ideas. This empowerment can lead to innovative solutions that management might not have considered.

- It could be impactful to encourage collaboration between different departments. Cross-functional teams bring diverse perspectives and can generate more innovative ideas.

- You can recognize and reward innovative ideas, even if they don't always succeed. This can be through formal recognition programs, bonuses, or simply public acknowledgment.

- You could bring some fun to the workplace atmosphere by sponsoring events like hackathons or innovation challenges. These events are effective in sparking creativity and can sometimes lead to practical solutions to real business challenges.

- Your employees would likely appreciate opportunities to learn all about new technologies and methodologies. You could support their interest through workshops, seminars, or online courses.

- You can let your staff and employees know they're in a safe environment where taking calculated risks is encouraged. This will help ensure that the fear of failure does not stifle creativity.

- You can establish open communication channels where employees at all levels can submit their ideas and feedback.

- You can occasionally look outside your industry for inspiration. Sometimes the most innovative ideas come from adapting solutions from other sectors.

By implementing these strategies, a company can cultivate a culture where innovation is not just a buzzword but a true driver of the everyday workflow.

But of course, none of this is possible without some risk. Mitigating risks is crucial in business, especially when adapting to changing environments. This involves identifying potential risks, assessing their likelihood and impact, and implementing strategies to minimize their effects.

A risk assessment process might involve the following steps:

- Identifying all potential risks that could impact the business, which can include financial risks, operational risks, market risks, environmental risks, and legal risks.

- Once risks are identified, analyzing them to understand their nature, cause, and potential impact. This can involve qualitative methods like brainstorming sessions or quantitative methods like statistical analysis.

- Assessing the likelihood of each risk occurring and its potential impact on the business. This step helps in prioritizing concerns.

- Developing a response strategy for each risk. This could involve risk avoidance, reduction, transfer (through insurance), or acceptance.

- Implementing risk response strategies and continuously monitoring the effectiveness of those measures.

- Regularly reviewing the risk assessment process and updating it to reflect an awareness of new risks or of changes in existing risks.

Effective risk assessment requires a systematic approach and would work best as an ongoing process, not a one-time activity.

To reduce risks that emerge with innovation, you can conduct thorough risk assessments to understand potential challenges and their impacts on the business. You can also develop contingency plans for different risk scenarios, creating strategies to address these risks before they materialize.

It's wise to continuously monitor market trends and internal processes, to identify new risks as rapidly as they emergee. Technology can help you predict, monitor, and manage risks effectively, and you can also train your employees to recognize and manage risks in their areas of operation.

Another way to lessen the risk that accompanies the creative approach is to diversify your products, services, and markets, which prevents too much risk from being concentrated in one area.

Incorporating Global Views: Expanding Horizons in Decision-Making

The necessity of considering global viewpoints has become obvious for companies plying their trade in the modern milieu. In The Moment, where decisions can have far-reaching consequences, understanding and integrating a global perspective is not just advantageous, it's imperative. This approach aligns with the evidence-over-emotion principle, ensuring that decisions are informed by a broad, worldly perspective rather than a narrow, localized viewpoint.

The Importance of Global Views

Given globalization, events in one part of the world can have ripple effects elsewhere. Understanding these global interconnections is crucial for making informed decisions that account for these potential impacts.

Global views bring diverse insights and ideas, enriching the decision-making process with varied cultural, economic, and geopolitical perspectives. In addition, incorporating global views helps in developing cultural sensitivity, an essential aspect in today's diverse world. This sensitivity is key to navigating modern international relations and global markets, and to working with multicultural teams.

For businesses hoping to remain competitive in an increasingly international marketplace, a global perspective is crucial. It helps in identifying global trends, understanding international consumer behavior, and spotting emerging opportunities.

Case Study: Google's Approach to a Global Marketplace

Google, which was founded in 1998 by Larry Page and Sergey Brin at Stanford University, started as a research project. But the company quickly evolved from a mere search engine into a multifaceted technology giant. Its iconic algorithm, PageRank, transformed how information is accessed and organized online.

Over the years, Google has not only dominated as a search engine but also expanded its portfolio to include a suite of collaboration tools like Google Drive, Google Docs, Gmail, and Google Meet, significantly impacting the way people communicate and work.

Its growth into other sectors such as mobile technology (Android OS), smart home devices (Google Home), and even self-driving cars (Waymo) highlights its capacity for innovation and adaptation. Google's success is also attributed to its strategic acquisitions, such as YouTube and Waze, which further diversified its offerings.

One of the touchstones of Google's enduring success has been its ability to adapt to the global marketplace. This includes localizing its search engine to cater to different linguistic and cultural contexts, ensuring compliance with regional legal and privacy standards, and continuously updating its algorithms and services to remain relevant and useful worldwide. This localization extends to services like Google Maps and Google News, which are tailored to deliver region-specific content.

Additionally, Google's commitment to cultural sensitivity has been crucial in maintaining its global dominance. This involves understanding and respecting cultural nuances, which has helped Google in developing products and services that resonate with a global audience.

Furthermore, Google's collaborative tools have revolutionized workplace communication, making it possible for teams worldwide to work together seamlessly. The integration of AI and machine learning into its services, from search algorithms to automated responses in Gmail, shows Google's commitment to continuous innovation and improvement.

Google's journey from a Stanford University project to a global tech leader is marked by constant innovation, strategic expansion, and an ability to adapt to an ever-changing digital landscape. This adaptability, combined with a commitment to meeting the diverse needs of a global audience, has ensured Google's position as a leading technology company.

Strategies for Incorporating Global Views

It is in every organization's interest to leverage globalization in any way they can. This means taking it seriously as a lasting trend and figuring out exactly how to use that understanding to your advantage.

This can be done by building teams with members from various cultural and geographical backgrounds. This diversity naturally brings global perspectives into discussions and decision-making. A further empowering step is to establish networks and partnerships with organizations and professionals around the world. These connections provide valuable insights into global trends and practices.

With globalization here to stay, you should probably consider it essential to stay informed about global events, trends, and shifts. This can be accomplished if you closely follow international news, read reports and journals that cover such events, and attend global conferences either virtually or in-person.

At a practical level, you can also invest in cross-cultural training and education for your team. Since understanding different cultural nuances and global dynamics is crucial for effective communication and decision-making, the consequences of this can only be positive.

To gain more in-depth knowledge about relevant issues, you can consult with international experts and advisors who can provide insights into global markets, policies, and cultural practices. You can also utilize technology to access global data and insights, depending on tools like international market analysis software, social media listening tools, and global consumer surveys to provide you with valuable information.

Incorporating global views is about ensuring that decisions are not only informed by a comprehensive understanding of the global landscape, but are also responsive to its complexities and nuances. You should recognize that in our interconnected world, a decision made in one corner can resonate across the globe, and thus must be made with a broad, inclusive perspective.

Objective Analysis in Summary

Concluding this chapter on objective analysis, we should re-emphasize the importance of a disciplined, evidence-based approach to decision-making, particularly in the high-stakes moments that define organizational trajectories.

Objective analysis, stripped of emotional bias and rooted in factual data, provides the clarity and precision necessary for effective leadership. As we transition to the dynamics of assembling a team in the next chapter, we will build on this foundation, exploring how the principles of objective analysis can be woven into team dynamics and leadership strategies. This will ensure that the teams we build and lead are as informed, adaptable, and resilient as the decisions they are tasked to make.

Questions about Objective Analysis

You can bring clarity to your study of objective analysis, and its relevance to your organization, by contemplating the following questions:

1. How does the chapter define objective analysis and why is it considered a survival skill in today's fast-paced world?

2. What are the three fundamental principles mentioned in this chapter that will allow you to master objective analysis?

3. Can you describe why prioritizing evidence over emotion is

crucial in objective analysis? See if you can give an example of a situation where this principle would be applied.

4. Why are diverse perspectives important in objective analysis? How do they contribute to the decision-making process?

5. Can you explain the significance of continuous reevaluation or the questioning of assumptions in objective analysis, especially in the context of rapidly changing information?

6. What are some of the challenges mentioned in the chapter in regard to practicing objective analysis in today's information-overloaded world?

7. How does objective analysis play a role in high-stakes scenarios, whether they occur in boardrooms or conflict zones?

8. Why is discipline and emotional detachment necessary for objective analysis? How does it impact decision-making?

9. Can you describe how objective analysis helps in navigating complex situations and making informed decisions?

10. How does objective analysis contribute to achieving clarity in complex scenarios?

11. How do the case studies mentioned in the chapter (e.g., Airbnb's adaptation during the Covid-19 pandemic) exemplify the application of Objective Analysis in real-world situations?

12. Is incorporating global views important in objective analysis, and how does it affect the decision-making process?

Assembling the Team

Now I'd like to focus on the profound impact that comes from assembling inclusive teams. In fact, this may be one of the most important aspects of Optimizing the Moment.

In The Moment, where decisions can shape futures and redefine paths, the composition of your team is imperative. Embracing inclusivity in team building aligns perfectly with the principle of evidence over emotion, ensuring decisions are made with the aid of a broad spectrum of insights and experiences.

The Essence of Inclusive Teams

Inclusive teams bring together a rich tapestry of backgrounds, experiences, and viewpoints. This diversity leads to a more holistic understanding of challenges and opportunities, providing a well-rounded foundation for decision making.

Diversity in teams naturally fosters innovation and creativity. Different perspectives often lead to unique solutions and approaches, challenging the status quo and sparking innovative ideas. Research consistently shows that inclusive teams perform better, as they are more engaged, more collaborative, and more committed to achieving their goals. Inclusivity not only enriches a team's work, but also strengthens their bond and commitment to the mission.

Throughout my career, I've learned how important it is to be sensitive to the diverse backgrounds and ideologies of team members. It's not just about their skills or resumes, it's about understanding the complex human dynamics at play when you interact with those who represent the full human spectrum of identities and experiences.

You should consider how different ideologies or ethnic backgrounds might interact within a team. This sensitivity is key to creating a cohesive and productive environment. Acknowledging and navigating the intricate tapestry of personal beliefs and experiences that each team member brings to the table is vital for forging deep connections reinforced by mutual respect and a shared sense of purpose.

This means we must recognize and honor the diverse ideologies of each team member. It's crucial to create a safe, open space where these differences can be respectfully discussed and understood. This not only fosters a more inclusive environment, but also strengthens our team's unity and effectiveness.

Strategies for Building Inclusive Teams

It isn't difficult to build inclusive teams if you make up your mind to do it. Building a diverse and inclusive team starts with an inclusive culture, and this means creating an environment where differences are respected, valued, and seen as a strength.

So how can you do this? Here are a few suggestions that have produced results for leaders in many organizations:

- You can encourage open dialogue, endorse mutual respect, and promote a sense of belonging among team members.

- You can actively seek diversity in the recruitment processes, by looking beyond the traditional talent pools and considering candidates from varied backgrounds and with different experiences and perspectives.

- You can enthusiastically encourage team members to share their viewpoints, and make it clear you expect these perspectives to be valued and considered. You can create platforms and forums where open and inclusive discussions can take place.

- You should try to provide all team members with equal access to opportunities for professional growth and development. This includes training, mentoring, and career advancement opportunities.

- As a leader, you can set the tone for inclusivity. You can demonstrate through your actions and decisions that inclusivity is a core value of the team, setting a powerful precedent in the process.

- You can continuously assess the team's dynamics and composition. If you do this you should be open to making adjustments to ensure the team remains diverse and inclusive, reflecting the changing nature of the workforce and society.

In the moments that matter, where each decision can have a profound impact, building inclusive teams is not just a moral imperative, it's also a strategic one. It ensures that decisions will be made with a depth of understanding, empathy, and creativity that can only come from a diverse and inclusive group of minds.

In these teams, every member will bring their unique perspective into a supportive environment where everyone feels valued, heard, and welcomed as an integral contributor to the success of the mission. This is the essence of effective leadership in today's complex and interconnected world.

Encouraging Openness and Inclusivity: Cultivating a Collaborative Environment in The Moment

Whether orchestrating initiatives in high-risk conflict zones or leading strategic discussions in boardrooms or with world leaders, one vital principle stands out, and that is the importance of fostering an environment defined by openness and inclusivity.

In The Moment, where decisions must be made swiftly yet remain grounded in sound reasoning, encouraging a culture where every voice is heard and valued is not just beneficial, it's essential. This practice aligns perfectly with the principle of evidence over emotion, creating an atmosphere where decisions are enriched with diverse viewpoints and collective wisdom.

Why Openness and Inclusivity are So Important

An open and inclusive environment acknowledges that great ideas can come from anyone, regardless of their rank or background. This recognition encourages all team members to contribute, leading to a richer pool of ideas and perspectives.

When team members feel their voices are heard and their contributions valued, it engenders trust and strengthens team cohesion. This sense of belonging is crucial for effective collaboration and teamwork.

Openness leads to a more comprehensive understanding of issues and challenges. Inclusivity ensures that decisions are made only after a wide range of experiences and insights have been considered, enhancing the quality, relevance, and effectiveness of those decisions.

Strategies for Encouraging Openness and Inclusivity

Knowing that openness and inclusivity have such an expansive upside, you will likely be ready to encourage them in your organization. Your efforts can be highly successful, if you follow at least some of these recommendations for action:

- You can make a big impression by being empathetic and practicing active listening. If you show (and feel genuine interest in) team members' ideas and concerns, this approach will set a tone that encourages open communication and mutual respect.

- You might establish forums where team members can freely express their thoughts and opinions without fear of judgment or repercussions. This could be regular team meetings, brainstorming sessions, or informal gatherings.

- You can actively encourage team members to share their unique perspectives. You can also challenge the team to consider issues from different angles and to think outside their usual paradigms.

- You can be as transparent as possible about decision-making processes, goals, and challenges facing your team or organization. This will pay dividends, since transparency produces an environment where trust is easily gained and more open communication is always encouraged.

- You can take it on yourself to recognize and celebrate the diverse backgrounds and experiences of team members. This acknowledgement can be expressed through team-building activities, diversity training, or simply through everyday interactions.

- You can ensure that all team members have an equal opportunity to participate and lead initiatives. Through careful observation you can become mindful of any biases that might prevent certain individuals from contributing.

In The Moment, encouraging openness and inclusivity is about creating a culture where every member of the team feels empowered to share their insights and ideas. It's about recognizing that the collective intelligence of a diverse and inclusive team is far greater than the sum of its parts.

Inclusivity not only enriches the decision-making process, but also cultivates a more dynamic, innovative, and resilient organization.

Once you've assembled your team, the next step is to make sure the effectiveness of that team is maximized as you move forward tackling many daunting challenges. The sections that follow will establish some guidelines that will help you improve teamwork, boost individual performance, and guarantee that everyone is on the same page and is working for the same cause.

Active Listening and Engagement: Essential Skills in The Moment

One thing I've come to recognize is that active listening and engagement are not just communication skills, but indispensable leadership tools. In The Moment—a critical juncture where any decision can have a profound impact—these skills ensure that we fully understand the situation and the thoughts and feelings of the people involved before we make a decision. This understanding is vital to making decisions grounded in evidence rather than emotion.

The Essence of Active Listening and Engagement

Perhaps you aren't 100% certain what the term 'active listening' actually means. If so, this breakdown should explain the concept:

Active listening goes beyond merely hearing the words. It also means understanding the message behind them, not in a shallow way but deeply and profoundly. Skilled active listeners pay attention to the speaker's tone, non-verbal cues, and emotions, and respond in a way that shows comprehension and empathy.

Engagement in this context means a two-way dialogue. Beyond just listening, you'll encourage your social partners to speak openly and to share their thoughts without inhibition, so they will feel heard. Such a dialogue helps create a deeper connection and increases mutual understanding.

By actively listening and engaging with team members, leaders build trust and respect. It demonstrates to the team that their opinions and insights are valued.

Strategies for Active Listening and Engagement

Active listening is a powerful communications tool. To cultivate a more effective active listening capacity, you can do the following:

- During conversations, to make a positive impression you can focus entirely on the speaker. To do this you must avoid distractions, maintain eye contact, and show that you are fully engaged in what they are saying.

- At various points during a conversation, you can paraphrase or summarize what you've heard to ensure you've understood correctly. You can ask clarifying questions to delve deeper into the speaker's point of view, and they will notice you're making an effort and really appreciate it.

- You should acknowledge that you understand and respect the speaker's feelings, even if you don't agree with their viewpoint. This validation shows empathy and a true regard for their perspective.

- You can take the time to respond to others in a thoughtful manner, showing that you have considered the speaker's ideas and are intrigued.

- In group settings, you can encourage input from all members, making certain that everyone has a chance to speak. You should be mindful of those who may be less inclined to speak up and invite their participation directly.
- You should be patient and try to keep an open mind. Active listening often requires withholding judgment and not jumping to conclusions or suggesting solutions too quickly.

In The Moment, active listening and engagement are more than just powerful communication techniques. They are also fundamental to understanding the full scope of a situation and can therefore help you make well-informed decisions. Active listening skills allow leaders to gather insights from a wide range of perspectives, leading to decisions that are not only more informed but also more inclusive and reflective of the collective intelligence of the team.

Continuous Re-evaluation: Dynamic Decision Making in The Moment

I have come to realize the immense value of continuous re-evaluation. In The Moment, the ability to continually reassess and adapt is not just advantageous, it's essential. This practice is a key aspect of ensuring that decisions are not just made based on evidence, but are also responsive to the fluidity of developments in an ever-changing landscape.

The Imperative of Continuous Re-evaluation

The only constant is change. Continuous re-evaluation allows us to adapt our strategies and decisions to align with evolving circumstances, be they market shifts, geopolitical changes, or alterations in internal organizational dynamics.

As new information becomes available, continuous re-evaluation enables us to refine and improve our strategies. This iterative process ensures that our actions are always consistent with and reliant on the most current and relevant data.

It's easy to become attached to a particular course of action, especially if it was based on a sound decision-making process. However, clinging to a decision without considering new information when it becomes available can lead to rigidity. Continuous re-evaluation prevents this from occurring, by encouraging a more flexible and responsive approach.

Strategies for Effective Continuous Re-evaluation

Continuous re-evaluation is the quintessential proactive strategy. As a standard operating procedure, it will give your organization an aggressive orientation, where you're always striving to stay one step ahead or remain on the cutting edge.

If you want to expand your use of continuous re-evaluation procedures, here are some ways you can do it:

- You can set up sessions at regular intervals to review decisions and strategies. This could happen weekly, monthly, or quarterly, depending on the nature of the decisions and the volatility of the environment.

- You can make an effort to keep abreast of new developments in your field, in the market, and in the geopolitical realm. This type of ongoing information gathering is crucial for informed re-evaluation.

- You can promote an organizational culture where change is not only accepted but embraced. You can openly encourage team members to bring new information to the table and be open to adjusting plans based on this data.

- You can implement feedback mechanisms to gather insights gleaned from your implementation of various decisions. You can use this feedback to inform the re-evaluation process.

- You may want to utilize data analytics tools to continuously monitor outcomes and key performance indicators. This real-time data can be invaluable for making smart and sensible adjustments.

- You can regularly engage in scenario planning to explore potential future developments and to see how they might impact current decisions. This forward-looking approach will help you stay prepared for different eventualities.

Continuous re-evaluation aligns with the principle of evidence over emotion by making certain that our decisions are not only based on the best available evidence at the time, but remain relevant and effective as circumstances evolve. This dynamic approach to decision-making is crucial for managing the complexities associated with modern leadership, where the ability to adapt and evolve is just as important as the ability to make sound initial decisions.

Navigating the Maze of Information: A Crucial Skill in The Moment

One of the most formidable challenges any organization will face in the modern age is navigating the sheer volume of information that is now available to help them make the best decisions.

During critical moments, information comes at you like a relentless storm. It creates a dense fog of data that can either confuse you or enlighten you, depending on how you sort through and process it, and on the strategies you use to separate the wheat from the chaff.

The Challenge of the Information Maze

We live in an era where information is abundant and access is almost instantaneous. The challenge lies not in obtaining information, but in sifting through it to find what's relevant. In The Moment, this challenge is amplified as you're often required to make swift decisions with potentially far-reaching consequences.

With the deluge of data comes the difficulty of discerning fact from fiction, or opinion from analysis. In critical decision-making scenarios, basing actions on inaccurate or misleading information can lead to disastrous outcomes. Too much information can lead to analysis paralysis, where the decision-making process is hindered by an overabundance of data. Finding a way to cut through the clutter to the heart of the matter is essential for effective action.

Strategies for Navigating the Maze

The information maze holds a lot of secrets that can help you out immensely, should you be able to discover them. Here's some advice for navigating that maze effectively, so you can exit with the data you need to make the best decisions for your organization:

- You can collaborate with your organizational partners to create a system to filter information efficiently. This could involve prioritizing sources based on reliability, setting up processes for quick validation of data, and identifying key indicators that are most relevant to your decision-making processes.

- You can take steps to make sure you have a team skilled in data analysis, one that is capable of quickly interpreting vast amounts of information and extracting what's pertinent. This team should be adept at using analytical tools and methodologies to distill data into actionable insights.

- In the face of overwhelming information, you can try to keep your objective in clear view. You can do this by continually asking, "Is this information relevant to our goal?" This focus makes it easier to discard extraneous data and concentrate on what's essential.

- You can utilize technology to manage and make sense of large data sets. Tools like data analytics software, AI, and machine learning can be invaluable in processing and analyzing information efficiently.

- You can try to develop and nurture the ability to make decisions swiftly based on the best available information. While it's important to be thorough, it's equally important to be timely, especially in situations where The Moment is fleeting.

- You can learn to recognize when information has become outdated. You can establish a routine for regularly updating your data and revising decisions as new information becomes available.

The ability to navigate a maze of information requires more than intellectual acumen. It's a learned, practical skill that can make the difference between a decision that is merely good and one that is truly great. It involves using evidence to cut through the noise, maintaining clarity of purpose and ensuring that every step taken is informed, deliberate, and focused on the end goal.

Deciphering Signals from Noise: A Key to Mastering The Moment

Throughout my life, I've come to recognize a fundamental truth: not all information holds equal value. The art of deciphering signals from noise is crucial, especially in The Moment, when making the right (or the wrong) decision can dramatically alter the course of events. Deciphering skills are essential for adhering to the principle of evidence over emotion, as they keep our decisions grounded in reality and prevent them from being obscured by irrelevant distractions.

Understanding Signals vs. Noise

Signals are the pieces of information that are directly relevant to your objectives. They are the insights, data points, and trends that align with your goals and provide actionable intelligence. In the cacophony of information, these are the notes that create harmony and direction.

Noise, on the other hand, is the surplus information that, while often interesting, is not directly relevant to the decision you are about to make. It's the background chatter that can distract from the real issues, leading to confusion and misdirection.

Strategies for Deciphering Signals from Noise

You can start making the distinction between signals and noise by having a crystal-clear understanding of your objectives. Knowing precisely what you are looking to achieve helps in identifying which information is a signal and which is just noise.

It can be most helpful to tailor your information-gathering methods to home in on the signals. This might involve setting specific criteria for what constitutes relevant data and being disciplined about not getting sidetracked by interesting but irrelevant information. To empower this deciphering process you can employ analytical tools and techniques to filter out noise. This could involve the use of data analysis software, statistical methods, or even algorithmic filtering, depending on the complexity and volume of the information you're analyzing.

As you move forward, you might want to consult with subject matter experts who can help in identifying which pieces of information are most critical. Their expertise can be invaluable in distinguishing between what is truly relevant and what is not.

It's important to recognize that the distinction between signal and noise can change over time as objectives evolve and new information becomes available. Consequently, you should regularly review your information filtering processes to ensure they remain in sync with your current objectives.

Your efforts to separate the signal from the noise will be more effective if you learn to practice mindful listening and observation. Often, the ability to pick up on the right signals is a matter of being attuned to subtle cues and patterns that might be overlooked in a more cursory review.

Deciphering signals from noise is akin to finding a guiding light in a storm. You can accomplish your mission by focusing on what truly matters, ensuring that every decision is based on information that is directly relevant and impactful. This skill requires analytical ability, but it's also a discipline, a way of engaging with the world that elevates the quality of our decisions, our strategies, and ultimately, our outcomes.

Understanding the Undercurrents: Navigating Hidden Dynamics in The Moment

Often what's visible on the surface only tells part of the story. In The Moment, understanding the undercurrents—those hidden dynamics and subtleties that influence events and decisions—is crucial. This depth of understanding is essential for making decisions that are not only informed but also insightful and effective.

The Significance of Undercurrents

Undercurrents represent the unseen forces at play in any complex undertaking. They are the cultural nuances, unspoken rules, hidden agendas, and emotional underpinnings that shape the environment and influence outcomes. As you might imagine, recognizing these elements is crucial for a complete understanding of any situation.

By comprehending and acknowledging the undercurrents, we can better predict the potential consequences of our decisions, including how they might be received and what ripple effects they might create. Grasping these underlying dynamics provides a strategic advantage, allowing for more nuanced and effective decision-making. Understanding these forces allows you to read between the lines and anticipate the deeper implications of actions and events.

Strategies for Understanding the Undercurrents

You can become a master at detecting the hidden or unacknowledged undercurrents if you apply at least some of these tips in your interactions with peers, partners, employees, and anyone else you encounter on a daily basis:

- You should try to pay close attention not just to what is said, but to how it is said, and to what is left unsaid. You should also observe body language, tone, and context. This kind of active listening and observation can reveal much about the underlying dynamics at play in any situation.

- You can try to deepen your understanding of the different cultural, social, and organizational contexts in which you operate. Empathy allows you to see things from others' perspectives, providing insights into motivations and concerns that might not be immediately apparent.

- Sometimes, the best way to understand the undercurrents is to engage directly with key stakeholders. Open and honest conversations with these individuals can uncover concerns and motivations that are not visible on the surface.

- Informal networks often hold the key to understanding the real dynamics within any group or organization. You can try to build relationships within these networks, since your interactions with individuals in this context can provide invaluable insights into   hidden truths.

- You can apply critical thinking to analyze the information gathered. You can combine this with intuition, which is an often-underestimated tool that can help you comprehend unspoken dynamics. Intuition, honed through experience and empathy, can be a powerful tool for reading the undercurrents.

- You may want to consult with a range of individuals from different backgrounds and areas of expertise. Their diversity of opinion can provide a more rounded understanding of the undercurrents that might be in play.

In those moments where decisions have profound implications, recognizing and understanding the undercurrents is a highly useful skill that functions as an essential aspect of leadership. It allows us to correctly read and interpret the complexities of human dynamics, ensuring that our decisions are made with a depth of understanding and awareness that goes beyond the obvious.

Achieving Clarity in Complexity

There are obstacles that can prevent you from interpreting complex situations correctly, which is necessary to achieve clarity of understanding. To solve this problem, I would recommend you implement some time-tested strategies that will help you reach the pinnacle of comprehension.

For example, you can employ structured analytical techniques to dissect the most complex scenarios. This could involve breaking the situation down into smaller and more comprehensible parts, conducting root cause analysis, or mapping out various scenarios and their potential outcomes. These techniques force us to move beyond superficial understanding and delve deeper into the core of the issue.

You can also encourage the development of a culture where critical thinking is praised and considered essential. You—and everyone else in your organization—should question every assumption, challenge conventional wisdom, and look at the situation from multiple angles. This kind of critical analysis is essential to achieving clarity, as it prevents you from relying on simplistic and emotion-driven conclusions.

To increase your range of perspectives, you should engage a diverse team in the analytical process. This will help because different perspectives can provide new insights and help uncover aspects of the situation that you might have missed. A collaborative approach ensures a more holistic understanding and helps in mitigating personal biases.

Part of achieving clarity is acknowledging what you don't know. In complex situations, uncertainty is a given. Instead of shying away from it, you can embrace it. You can use it as a motivating force for continuous learning and adaptation. Recognizing uncertainty helps in staying agile and responsive to new information as it emerges.

Clarity in complexity sounds like a catchphrase, but it's a vital component of effective leadership in The Moment. Finding clarity in complexity allows you to harness the power of evidence to properly decode the complicated nature of modern challenges. By embracing this approach, leaders can make decisions that are not just effective in the immediate context, but also sustainable and resilient in the long term.

Data-Driven Insights: The Keystone of Objective Decision Making

Given the warp speed at which the world operates, where The Moment can be both fleeting and fraught with consequences, data-driven insights stand as the bedrock of objective decision-making. As a cornerstone principle of evidence over emotion, relying on data-driven insights will help you channel the power of information into actionable wisdom.

Embracing Data-Driven Insights

I've learned that data is more than just numbers or statistics. It's a narrative waiting to be understood. Data-driven insights enable us to cut through biases and assumptions, providing a grounded, factual basis for our decisions.

Data reveals the past, but it also opens a window into the future. By analyzing trends and patterns, we can predict potential outcomes and make informed decisions that are proactive rather than reactive. This foresight is invaluable, especially in The Moment, where every decision can irrevocably alter the course of events.

Every challenge or opportunity is unique, and data allows us to tailor our approaches accordingly. By analyzing specific datasets relevant to the situation at hand, we can craft solutions that are not just effective but also efficient and targeted.

Implementing Data-Driven Insights

The first step to leveraging data-driven insights is to invest in robust data collection mechanisms. This involves not just collecting quantitative data, but also developing qualitative insights that can provide context and depth to the numbers.

Data is only as useful as our ability to analyze and interpret it. Building strong analytical capabilities within a team, whether through training or hiring expertise, is essential. This capability ensures that the organization doesn't just collect data but also understands and utilizes it effectively.

If you want to bring data analysis to the forefront, you should try to create a culture where decisions are made based on evidence and data, not on hunches or intuitions. This culture shift requires consistent reinforcement and a shared understanding of the value of data-driven insights.

The world of data collection is ever-evolving. Hence, a key aspect of implementing data-driven insights is the willingness to adapt and learn continuously. This adaptive approach keeps an organization agile and responsive to new information and changing circumstances.

In the pursuit of data-driven insights, it's crucial to uphold ethical standards and ensure data integrity. This means respecting privacy, ensuring the accuracy of data sources, and being transparent about how data is used in decision-making processes.

In The Moment, where the lines between success and failure and opportunity and risk are often razor-thin, data-driven insights provide the clarity and conviction needed to make informed decisions. They are the compass that guides us through the complexities of modern decision-making, ensuring that our choices are grounded in reality and therefore leave us poised for success.

Seeking Objective Counsel: Navigating The Moment with Unbiased Advice

One truth has been consistently clear: no one person has all the answers. In The Moment, where the consequences of decisions are amplified, seeking objective counsel is not just wise—it's essential. This practice is a bulwark against the tunnel vision that can come from relying solely on one's perspective or a homogeneous group's thoughts.

The Vital Role of Objective Counsel

Objective counsel brings in fresh perspectives, often challenging our ingrained thinking patterns. It can illuminate blind spots in our reasoning and introduce new ideas that we might not have considered.

We all have biases, shaped by our experiences, culture, ideology, politics, upbringing, and environment. Consulting with objective advisors helps counteract these biases, ensuring that decisions are not colored by personal prejudices or limited viewpoints.

Decisions made after consulting with a range of experts and stakeholders are generally more credible. This credibility is crucial, especially when decisions need to be explained and justified to a wider audience.

Strategies for Seeking Objective Counsel

Even after you've assembled a team full of smart, talented people whose perspectives complement each other well, you will still have use for objective counsel. Here's some advice on how you can fill that crucial need:

- You can build a network of experts and trusted advisors whose opinions you respect and who bring different viewpoints to the table. These could be mentors, industry experts, peers from different fields, or even academics.

- You can continue to cultivate an organizational culture where seeking advice is valued and encouraged. You may encourage team members at all levels to seek external opinions and to bring diverse insights back to the organization.

- If possible, you can set up an advisory board or consult with existing boards regularly. These boards should consist of individuals with varied backgrounds and expertise, offering a wide spectrum of insights.

- Sometimes the best counsel comes from outside your immediate industry. That's why you might want to search for insights from other sectors, where leaders face similar challenges or have gone through comparable transformations.

- While external advice is invaluable, it's also important to balance it with internal knowledge and insights. That's why you should take the outsider's perspective with a grain of salt, and always check to make sure that the advice you're receiving is contextualized to your specific situation and organization.

- Given the influence of technology on our everyday lives, objective counsel can also come from technological tools and data analytics. You can make good use of these resources to gather information and insights that can inform your decision-making.

Since each decision can have far-reaching implications, seeking objective counsel is a strategy that goes beyond mere risk mitigation. It's about embracing the power of collective wisdom, ensuring that decisions are well-rounded, informed, and as free from personal biases as possible. This approach not only strengthens the decision-making process, but also contributes to a more dynamic, informed, and resilient leadership style.

Stress-Testing Decisions: Ensuring Robustness in The Moment

Not all decisions that look good on paper will stand firm in the real world. This is where the concept of stress-testing becomes crucial. It's akin to putting your team's strategies through a series of trials, to see if they can withstand the unexpected twists and turns of real-world scenarios.

The Importance of Stress-Testing Decisions

Just like engineers test materials under physical stress to gauge their durability, stress-testing decisions involves putting your strategies and plans under hypothetical pressures to assess their resilience. This process uncovers potential weaknesses that might not be evident in a normal analysis.

The reality of The Moment is that it is often fraught with unforeseen circumstances. Stress testing helps in preparing for these eventualities, ensuring that your decisions are not just effective in ideal conditions, but also in less predictable situations.

By understanding how decisions might play out under different scenarios, you can build adaptability and flexibility into your plans. This foresight is invaluable in a world where change is the only constant.

How to Effectively Stress-Test Decisions

Stress-testing protocols are generally based on proven methods for detecting hidden or overlooked complications or difficulties. What follows are a few of these proven methods, which can help you sharpen your stress-testing procedures:

- You can create a range of 'what-if' scenarios for each major decision. These scenarios should cover possible changes in the market, shifts in stakeholder attitudes, technological disruptions, geopolitical upheavals, and even internal organizational changes.

- You can recruit cross-functional teams to participate in the stress-testing process. Different departments can provide insights into how a decision might impact various aspects of the organization.

- Sometimes, internal teams might be too close to a project to see potential flaws. For this reason, you may want to consider bringing in external consultants or advisors to handle or assist with your stress testing. They can provide a fresh perspective and help identify issues that internal teams might have overlooked.

- You can certainly learn a lot by using simulations and modeling tools to test how decisions might play out. These tools can provide a visual representation of potential outcomes and help in identifying areas where plans might need to be adjusted.

- You probably shouldn't look upon stress testing as a one-time exercise. Regular reviews and reassessments of your decisions can guarantee they will remain relevant and robust in the face of new information or changing circumstances.

Stress testing decisions represents a crucial step that can help you prove your choices are not just theoretically sound, but practically resilient. This approach puts your decision-making processes on firmer ground while also instilling a sense of confidence and preparedness, equipping you to maneuver through the complexities of our ever-changing world with a more strategic, informed, and dynamic mindset.

Assembling the Team: Creating a Cohesive Unit for The Moment

The art of assembling a team stands out as a crucial element of mission success. In The Moment, the act of bringing together individuals who may not know each other, and uniting them in pursuit of a common goal, is not just a task but a transformative endeavor.

This process goes beyond mere group formation. It means instilling a sense of purpose, aligning values, and fostering an environment where every member feels valued and empowered to contribute.

The Art of Team Assembly

Before assembling the team, you should clearly define the mission. Understanding the mission's objectives, challenges, and requirements is key to identifying the right mix of skills and personalities you'll need from team members.

You should look for individuals whose skills complement each other. On a well-rounded team, each member brings their unique strengths, which, when combined, creates a synergistic effect, enhancing the team's overall capability.

It is good practice to select team members who share core values and beliefs relating to the mission. This practice will ensure that everyone is working towards the same goal, driven by a sense of identical purpose.

From the earliest stage of the team-building process, you should strive to foster an environment where team members feel supported both by leadership and by each other. This support is crucial for encouraging open communication, collaboration, and mutual respect.

As your collaborative work progresses, you should make it a practice to recognize and celebrate the contributions of each team member. Feeling valued and acknowledged boosts morale and motivates individuals to invest their best effort to complete every assigned task.

You should try to assemble a team that is not just skilled, but also eager to learn and grow. A team that views challenges as opportunities for development will be more adaptive and resilient in the face of adversity.

Finally, you should encourage team members to build relationships with each other. Strong interpersonal connections enhance trust and understanding and create a sense of camaraderie, all of which are vital for a cohesive team.

Practical Steps in Team Assembly

Mastering the mechanics of assembling a dynamic team can be challenging. But here is where you can put what you've learned through your history of leadership into practice.

Some of the best ideas for creating an enduring and effective team include:

- Embracing diversity in its broadest sense—cultural, experiential, cognitive—to bring a wealth of perspectives and ideas to the table.

- Having a structured onboarding process that helps new members understand the team's mission, values, and working style, ensuring they feel integrated from the start.

- Regularly engaging in team-building activities that are not just fun but also revealing, helping members to understand each other's strengths, weaknesses, and working preferences.

- Creating opportunities for team members to openly discuss ideas, challenges, and feedback. This could be through regular meetings, brainstorming sessions, or informal gatherings.

- Practicing a leadership style that empowers team members, giving them autonomy and responsibility and encouraging them to take ownership of their roles.

- Establishing clear conflict resolution mechanisms. A team with diverse viewpoints might face conflicts, and having a process to address and resolve these respectfully is crucial.

The process of assembling a team will be a microcosm of the mission itself. You'll be trying to create a unit where diverse skills, perspectives, and personalities converge toward a common goal. It's about nurturing a space where each member not only contributes to the mission, but also grows, learns, and thrives. This is the essence of building a team that is not just effective but also resilient, adaptive, and fully committed to the mission.

Defining the Mission in the Context of Assembling the Team

I have spoken quite a bit about defining the mission. In the context of assembling the team, let's discuss it in more detail.

I've observed that the clarity and purpose of the mission are paramount, and this clarity becomes particularly crucial when assembling a team. The mission not only guides the selection of team members, but also serves as the unifying force that binds them together. In The Moment, the mission is the beacon that illuminates the path for the team, directing their collective efforts and energies.

Integrating the Mission into Team Assembly

The mission statement should clearly articulate the goals, values, and purpose of the endeavor. It acts as the guiding light, ensuring that every team member understands and aligns with what the team aims to achieve.

When assembling the team, each member's skills and expertise should be aligned with specific aspects of the mission. This alignment will ensure that the team has the necessary capabilities to meet the mission's objectives.

The values inherent in the mission should be reflected in the team's composition. Selecting team members who share these values fosters a strong, cohesive unit that is collectively committed to achievement.

The mission should be compelling enough to motivate and inspire the team. A well-defined mission can ignite passion and commitment in team members, pushing them to go beyond their limits.

In some cases, the mission might require team members to adapt to roles or responsibilities that are new or challenging. A clear understanding of the mission can encourage team members to embrace these changes willingly.

When team members are involved in defining or interpreting the mission, it encourages a sense of ownership and responsibility towards achieving its goals.

Practical Implications in Team Assembly

During the recruitment and onboarding process, you should clearly communicate the goals and parameters of the mission. This helps potential team members understand what they are committing to and what that commitment will entail.

The interview process can be devoted to assessing how well candidates' values and motivations match the purpose of the mission. You can ask questions that will reveal their comprehension of and dedication to the mission's goals.

As the mission continues, you can conduct regular team briefings and workshops focused on its requirements. This will keep the team aligned and focused throughout the project lifecycle. In general you will want to foster an environment where team members can discuss how their work contributes to the mission. This can lead to new insights and reinforce their commitment.

To help team members stay on track, you can establish feedback mechanisms focused exclusively on the mission's progress. Regular feedback will help team members understand how their contributions are advancing the mission, or failing to advance the mission if there are difficulties.

Defining the mission and integrating it into the process of assembling the team is about creating a shared sense of purpose and direction. It's about ensuring that every member of the team is not just technically equipped, but also emotionally and intellectually invested in everything your team is doing. This unified focus on the mission is what drives a team and enables it to achieve extraordinary results.

Identifying the Mission: Setting the Cornerstone for Strategic Success

Accurately identifying the mission is the first and most critical step. The mission acts as the cornerstone, setting the direction and tone for all subsequent actions. In The Moment, where every decision can have far-reaching implications, a well-defined mission is both a statement of intent and a blueprint for action.

The Process of Identifying the Mission

You can begin zeroing in on the specifics of the mission by ensuring everyone thoroughly understands the environment in which the mission will operate. This includes assessing the current situation, identifying challenges and opportunities, and understanding the broader context, in all of its geopolitical, economic, social, and technological aspects.

A key question to ask is, 'what are the primary goals we aim to achieve?' You should try to define these goals clearly and make sure they are achievable and measurable. Objectives should be specific, relevant to the appropriate context, and aligned with the overarching purpose.

Of course, you should always try to make sure the mission will promote and demonstrate your organization's core values. This is crucial for maintaining integrity and authenticity throughout the pursuit of the mission.

To get everyone on board, you can engage with key stakeholders, team members, experts, and possibly external advisors to gain multiple perspectives. This collaborative approach can provide valuable insights and will help in refining the mission's components.

When you're finally ready to put it into written and/or spoken form, the mission should be articulated in a clear, concise, and compelling manner. It should inspire action and commitment among those involved. While clarity is important, the mission should also have room for adaptation. In a rapidly changing environment, the ability to pivot and adjust the mission as needed is essential.

Practical Considerations in Mission Identification

During the mission refinement stage, you can take several steps to make sure the mission is well-conceived and well-articulated:

- Conducting a Strengths, Weaknesses, Opportunities, and Threats (SWOT) analysis could be quite helpful, as it could give you a more comprehensive understanding of the internal and external factors that could impact the mission.

- You should try to understand who the mission stakeholders are and what their interests and needs might be. Stakeholder analysis can help in crafting a mission that addresses key concerns and garners broad support.

- While the mission should be ambitious, you certainly should be careful to set realistic expectations. Overly ambitious missions can lead to disappointment and a loss of motivation.

- Once the mission is identified, you can communicate it effectively to all involved parties. Clear communication ensures everyone is on the same page and working towards a common goal.

- You can regularly reevaluate the progress and parameters of the mission to keep it relevant and effective. This re-evaluation is particularly important in dynamic environments, where changes can be rapid and unpredictable.

In The Moment, identifying the mission is about establishing a clear, strategic, and purpose-driven path forward. It's about setting a direction that is not only focused on achieving specific goals, but is also resonant with the values and aspirations of everyone involved. A well-identified mission keeps all efforts aligned and focused toward achieving the desired outcome.

Seeking Complementary Skills: Enhancing Team Efficacy in The Moment

In The Moment, where every decision can lead to significant outcomes, having a team whose skills complement each other is not just beneficial; it's essential for success. This approach resonates with the evidence-over-emotion philosophy, as it guarantees the team will be well-equipped to handle diverse aspects of a mission, with each member bringing their unique strengths to the table.

Why Complementary Skills are Crucial

A team blessed with people who possess complementary skills will display a broader range of abilities and expertise. This diversity will be vital for addressing various facets of a mission, from analytical thinking to creative problem-solving, and from technical know-how to planning.

When team members have different, yet complementary skills, they can tackle problems more effectively. Each member views challenges from their unique perspective, leading to more innovative and comprehensive solutions.

Teams with complementary skills tend to have balanced dynamics. Members can support and learn from each other, fostering an environment of mutual respect and collaboration. Teams that possess a variety of skills are generally more flexible and adaptable. They can pivot and respond to changing circumstances more effectively, a critical ability in dynamic environments.

By leveraging the unique strengths of each team member, the overall potential of the team will be maximized. This leads to higher productivity, better decision-making, and more successful outcomes.

Strategies for Seeking Complementary Skills

So how can you make sure that your team will be comprised of individuals with diverse and complementary skills? Here are a few team-building steps that will help you secure this outcome:

- You can list the skills required for the mission and map out the existing skills your team members possess. You can then identify any gaps and seek new members who can offer the missing skill sets.

- It could be a great idea to focus on diversity in recruitment. You can look for candidates from different backgrounds, industries, and areas of expertise to bring a rich mix of skills to the team.

- You can conduct regular team assessments to more fully understand the strengths and weaknesses of each member. Going forward you can use this information to guide team development and task allocation.

- You may want to encourage cross-training within the team. This not only helps in building complementary skills, but also promotes a deeper understanding and appreciation of each other's roles.

- While having fixed roles can be helpful, if you have a talented team you can preserve some flexibility in roles so that team members can apply their skills where most needed, especially in response to evolving project demands.

- It could be wise to invest in the continuous development of team members' skills. This could be through training programs, workshops, or mentorship opportunities.

Seeking complementary skills means you'll be strategically assembling a team that collectively possesses the capabilities to handle complex situations and achieve the mission's goals. It's about recognizing that the collective strength of a diverse skill set is greater than the sum of its parts, and leveraging this insight to its fullest potential.

Aligning Values with the Mission: Creating a Unified Purpose

The alignment of values with the mission is not just beneficial. It's essential for meaningful and sustained success. This alignment forms the backbone of any endeavor, especially in critical moments where every decision and action can have significant consequences. In the ethos of 'evidence over emotion,' aligning values with the mission ensures that every team member is not only working towards the same goal, but is also intrinsically motivated by a shared set of beliefs and principles.

The Importance of Values-Mission Alignment

When team members share common values that fit the mission like a glove, they are bound by a collective purpose. This shared purpose acts as a powerful motivator and unifier, ensuring that everyone is striving toward the same amazing end result. Reaching this level of integration will foster trust, mutual respect, and a sense of belonging, which are vital for effective teamwork, especially in challenging situations.

Aligned values ensure that decisions made by different team members are consistent with the overall mission. This consistency is crucial in maintaining strategic direction and integrity in action. Teams united by common values and a shared sense of purpose are certainly more resilient in the face of adversity, since they can draw strength from their shared commitment to overcoming even the most formidable of challenges.

People are drawn to organizations and missions that resonate with their personal values. Alignment in this area is key to attracting and retaining top talent.

Strategies for Aligning Values and Mission

As you prepare your team for action, you can articulate the values and mission clearly and ensure they are communicated effectively to all team members. This clarity helps in ensuring that everyone understands and is on the same page.

During the recruitment process, you should assess candidates not just for skills, but also for value alignment. This helps in building a team that is naturally inclined to work cooperatively toward the completion of the mission. Shared values can be embedded into everyday operations, decision-making processes, and organizational culture. You can make them a living embodiment of what the organization stands for, meaning they won't be just a statement on the wall.

While understanding everyone's sincere intentions, you probably shouldn't take anything for granted. You should encourage regular reflection and dialogue about how the team's actions and decisions are aligning with the values and the mission at the present moment. This keeps value alignment at the forefront of everyone's consciousness. Concurrently you can create mechanisms for feedback on how well the values and mission are being upheld, and be open to making adaptations as required.

It is vital that leaders exemplify the values and mission in their actions and decisions. Leading by example is one of the most powerful ways to reinforce their importance, and it can be quite inspirational to team members as well.

Aligning values with the mission creates a deep-seated synergy between what the team believes in and what it aims to achieve. Making this a priority guarantees that every step taken will be both strategically sound and ethically and morally grounded. This alignment is the key to building a team that is not only effective in achieving its goals, but also consistent in its approach and resilient in its capacity to overcome obstacles that arise along its journey.

Questions about Assembling the Team

Given the density and importance of this chapter, I have broken up the questions to ponder into sections:

1. Understanding Inclusive Teams:
- What are the key benefits of having an inclusive team?
- How does diversity in a team foster innovation and creativity?
- Can you explain how inclusive teams enhance overall team performance and engagement?

2. Strategies for Building Inclusive Teams:
- What strategies does the chapter suggest for prioritizing diversity in recruitment?
- How can a leader create an inclusive culture within their team?
- Can you explain the importance of providing equal opportunities for growth and development in a team?

3. Active Listening and Engagement:
- What is the difference between hearing and understanding in the context of active listening?
- How does active listening and engagement contribute to building trust and respect in a team?
- What are some strategies a leader can use to practice active listening and engagement?

4. Continuous Reevaluation in Decision-Making:
- Why is continuous reevaluation important in dynamic decision-making scenarios?
- What are some effective strategies for continuous reevaluation in a team setting?

- How does continuous reevaluation help in adapting to changing circumstances?

5. Navigating the Information Maze:
- What challenges does a leader face while navigating through a large volume of information?
- How can a leader develop an efficient filtering mechanism to manage information effectively?
- Why is it important to separate fact from fiction and avoid analysis paralysis?

6. Deciphering Signals from Noise:
- Can you explain the concept of 'signals' and 'noise' in the context of team decision-making?
- What strategies can be employed to effectively decipher signals from noise?
- How does clarity of objectives help in identifying relevant information?

7. Understanding the Undercurrents:
- Why is it important to understand the undercurrents in team dynamics?
- What are some strategies you can use to navigate hidden dynamics and undercurrents within a team?
- How does understanding undercurrents contribute to strategic advantage in decision-making?

8. Team Assembly and Mission Alignment:
- What factors should be considered when identifying the mission in the context of assembling a team?

- Why is the alignment of team members' values with the mission so vital?
- How can a leader ensure that the mission is integrated into the team assembly process?

9. Seeking Complementary Skills:
- Why are complementary skills crucial in a team?
- What approaches can be taken to ensure a team has a balanced set of complementary skills?
- How does having diverse skills in a team enhance problem-solving and flexibility?

10. Leadership and Team Cohesion:
- What role does leadership play in fostering a supportive environment for the team?
- How can a leader encourage learning and growth within the team?
- Why is it important to recognize and celebrate individual contributions when you have a team?

Communicating the Mission

The power of effectively communicating the mission should be evident. It's not just about what the mission is, but also about how, why, when, and to whom it is communicated. These elements are crucial for ensuring that everyone involved understands, embraces, and supports the mission with 100% enthusiasm.

How to Communicate about the Mission

As you explain the outline and characteristics of a mission, your words should be easy to understand. You should try to avoid jargon and complex language, so the mission will seem clear and straightforward (as it actually should be).

To make sure everyone understands, you should communicate consistently across all platforms and during all interactions. Consistent messaging will reinforce the importance of the mission and help it to become ingrained within the minds of your team members. You can also use storytelling to make the mission more relatable and engaging, as a compelling narrative will help people connect with the mission on a deeper level.

One way to ensure comprehension and engagement is to utilize visual aids in your presentations, such as diagrams or infographics, to convey the fundamentals of the mission. Interactive sessions, like workshops or team-building exercises, can also help increase comprehension of the mission's purpose.

Clarity and Simplicity in Communicating the Mission

I have found that the essence of effective communication lies in clarity and simplicity. This is particularly true when articulating a mission. The mission should be presented in a manner that is easily understandable and memorable, ensuring that every team member, regardless of their background or expertise, can grasp it and choose their actions accordingly.

Why Clarity and Simplicity are Essential

A clear and simple mission statement can be understood by everyone involved, from the executive team to new employees. It transcends jargon and technical language, making it universally accessible. Clarity involves stripping down the mission to its core elements. This focus allows team members to quickly understand the mission's primary objectives without being overwhelmed by unnecessary details.

Simplicity in communication means that the mission can be easily conveyed and reiterated across different channels and settings. It aids in reinforcing the message without causing confusion or misinterpretation.

A mission that is clear and simple is easier to remember and act upon. The clarity facilitates full alignment of actions and decisions with the mission's objectives.

Implementing Clarity and Simplicity

Making the mission comprehensible and therefore motivating requires a customized approach to communication.

You should probably avoid the temptation to include too many elements or complex language in the mission statement. You should keep it concise and focused, utilizing plain language that can be easily understood. This doesn't mean oversimplifying to the point of losing meaning, but it does mean avoiding unnecessary technical jargon or corporate speak.

Regularly repeating your descriptions of the mission in various communications can be a good strategy, since it will help embed the mission in the team's collective consciousness. You can imprint it into their minds even more effectively by employing visual aids or analogies that relate to the mission. These can be powerful tools in making complex ideas more tangible and relatable.

You can place a special focus on the mission during training and onboarding programs. This will be a way of introducing new team members to the mission, in a way that is clear and straightforward.

Examples of Clarity and Simplicity in Action

Clarity and simplicity should guide your hand as you compose a mission statement that is concise and to the point, and that encapsulates the core purpose of the team or project.

Designing brochures, posters, or digital content that clearly and simply communicates the mission using easy-to-understand language and visuals is yet another example that will illustrate your commitment to making everything clear and transparent.

When you discuss the mission in team meetings, as you should do regularly, you should try to do so in a straightforward manner, ensuring that it's well understood and always at the forefront of your planning sessions.

Consistency in Communicating the Mission: A Pillar of Strategic Execution

Consistency in communicating the mission is not just beneficial—it's crucial. It ensures that the mission remains clear and unaltered in its core message across all levels and times, providing a stable and reliable foundation for decision-making, team alignment, and strategic execution.

The Crucial Role of Consistency

Consistency in the mission's communication ensures that everyone understands and remembers the primary goal. It prevents deviations and keeps all efforts aligned with the core objectives.

When the mission is communicated with consistency, it builds trust among team members and stakeholders. They know what to expect and can rely on the steady direction of their leaders.

Among its other benefits, consistent communication provides a stable framework for decision-making. Team members can make informed decisions knowing they align with the unchanging mission. Inconsistent messaging, on the other hand, can lead to confusion and misinterpretation of the mission, diluting its effectiveness and potentially leading to conflicting actions.

Implementing Consistency in Communication

If you don't have a plan to guarantee you stay on message at all times, your efforts to be consistent in your communications about the mission may be thwarted. With that in mind, here is a plan of attack that should help you avoid inconsistency:

- You can develop a standardized version of the mission statement and key messages, while taking steps to see that it is used across all communication platforms.

- You can use various communications formats—meetings, emails, reports, etc.—to reinforce the true meaning and purpose of the mission. This repetition will help keep the mission and its parameters front-and-center at all times.

- Leadership can make a concerted effort to remain steadfast in how they communicate about the mission. Mixed messages from different leaders can cause tremendous confusion in a short period of time.

- You can provide training and resources to team members to help them understand and communicate the mission consistently, if you have any reason to believe this might be a problem.

- You can implement vigorous feedback mechanisms to monitor whether the mission is being communicated and understood consistently. You can adjust your strategies as needed based on this feedback.

- You can recognize and reward team members when they perform at a high level while aligning their actions and decisions with the mission. This encourages consistent behavior that will support the mission and bring it to completion more quickly.

Examples of Consistency in Action

Whether in internal memos or external presentations, the mission should be articulated in a uniform manner, so that everyone receives the same message.

In the meantime, leaders can consistently emphasize the mission in their communications, using it as a central reference point for decision-making and strategic discussions.

Another way to demonstrate consistency is to incorporate the mission into training programs. This will ensure that new team members receive the same instructions as more established team members, right from the beginning of their education.

Incorporating Storytelling While Communicating the Mission

Time and time again, I have observed the profound impact that storytelling can have in clarifying, humanizing, and energizing a mission. Storytelling transcends mere data and facts; it connects on a human level, making the mission relatable, memorable, and inspiring. It's a method that brings the mission to life, creating a narrative that people can connect with emotionally and intellectually.

The Power of Storytelling

Stories have the ability to evoke emotions and create a personal connection with the audience. They can inspire, motivate, and engage in ways that facts and figures alone cannot. A well-told story can simplify complex concepts, making them more understandable and relatable. It can provide context and meaning to the mission, making it more accessible.

Humans are naturally wired to remember stories. By embedding the mission in a narrative, you make it more memorable, ensuring it stays in the minds of your audience. Stories create a sense of shared experience, building a community around the mission. They can unite diverse individuals in a group under a common umbrella of comprehension.

Through storytelling, you can illustrate past successes, vividly describe how challenges were overcome, and highlight the exciting developments that defined a mission's journey to completion. This will add depth and credibility to your message.

Implementing Storytelling in Mission Communication

But how exactly can you incorporate storytelling into your presentations about the mission? Here's how you can accomplish this:

- You can try to develop a narrative around the mission that includes elements such as the mission's origin, its significance, challenges faced, and successes achieved.

- You can include stories and anecdotes about real-life occurrences that exemplify the mission. This could include stories about team members or beneficiaries of the mission, or historical analogies that convey the proper message.

- You can enhance your stories with visual aids, such as images or videos, and other sensory elements to make them more engaging and impactful.

- You can provide training and resources to leaders and communicators in the art of storytelling. Fortunately, effective storytelling is a skill that can be developed and refined.

- You can try to foster an environment where team members are encouraged to share their own stories, especially the ones that somehow relate to the mission. The team could then be exposed to a rich tapestry of narratives that ultimately support the mission and its objectives.

- Telling stories that align with and reinforce the core messages of the mission can be extremely provocative and effective. The messages in these stories should be consistent with your overall strategic objectives.

Storytelling in Action

Leaders use storytelling in their speeches to illustrate the mission's importance and impact, making abstract concepts tangible and inspiring.

Those who are most skilled at it will integrate stories into their marketing materials, like brochures or videos, to convey the mission in a relatable and engaging way. They will share stories in internal communications, through newsletters or intranet, for example, to reinforce the mission and celebrate achievements within the organization.

Using Visual and Interactive Elements in Mission-Related Communications

I've seen the profound impact that visual and interactive elements can have in communicating a mission. They do not just convey information; they engage the senses, create lasting impressions, and foster interactive understanding.

Visuals such as images, charts, and videos capture attention more effectively than text alone. They can make the communication more engaging and interesting. Complex ideas can be simplified through visual representation. Diagrams, infographics, and models can help in breaking down complex concepts into understandable parts, which is why I've learned to use them whenever appropriate.

People tend to remember visual information better than text. Visual elements can make the mission more memorable and easier to recall. As a result, interactive elements like workshops, simulations, and group discussions can lead to a deeper understanding of the mission. They encourage active participation and hands-on learning. Interactive sessions can create a sense of collaboration and team spirit. They bring people together to discuss, explore, and internalize the mission.

Implementing Visual and Interactive Communication

If you want to add this kind of supplemental material to your written or spoken presentations, you have a number of options available:

- You can employ a variety of visual aids, including charts, graphs, infographics, videos and animations, to illustrate different aspects of the mission.

- You may want to organize interactive workshops and seminars where team members can engage with the mission in a hands-on manner. In these meetings you can include activities that encourage discussion and exploration of the mission's principles.

- If it suits your communication style, you can use gamification techniques, such as quizzes, puzzles, or role-playing games, to make learning about the mission fun and engaging.

- You can combine storytelling with visual elements. You can use visual storytelling techniques, like photo essays or short films, to narrate the mission's story.

- You should regularly update the team with visual content related to the mission, such as dashboards showing progress or visuals celebrating milestones.

- If you want to be especially creative, you can introduce team members to immersive experiences like virtual reality (VR) or augmented reality (AR) simulations, which will allow them to experience aspects of the mission in a more lifelike manner.

Visual and Interactive Elements in Action

Many organizations use well-designed PowerPoint presentations or videos in meetings to communicate about their mission more effectively. Some will also conduct team-building activities that revolve around the mission, helping team members understand and internalize it. Another popular strategy is to utilize digital platforms, like intranets or specialized apps, to create an interactive space for team members to learn about and engage with the mission.

Why Communicating the Mission is So Essential

Communicating the mission effectively helps in building a shared sense of purpose among team members and stakeholders. It points everyone toward a common goal.

In addition, a well-communicated mission can motivate and inspire those who become involved. It can act as a driving force that energizes and encourages the team to strive for excellence.

Clear communication of the mission should guide decision-making at all levels. It will ensure that decisions are routinely in harmony with your overarching goal.

When to Communicate the Mission

You may be wondering about when the time is right to communicate about the mission. Generally speaking, you should probably introduce the mission at the very beginning of any initiative or project. This sets the tone and direction right from the start.

Regardless of when communication starts, you should remind everyone of what the mission is all about at regular intervals, to keep this information fresh in everyone's mind. This can be done through meetings, newsletters, or regular updates. You should be especially diligent about reminding everyone of what the mission entails when you reach critical decision points, or are facing significant challenges. This can provide clarity and focus during tough times.

Who Needs to Know about the Mission?

You should take steps to confirm that every team member, regardless of their role, understands the mission. This includes new hires who need to be brought up to speed. You should also communicate the mission to all stakeholders, including investors, partners, and clients. This helps build trust and secure consent from all affected parties.

Depending on the nature of the mission, it may also be important to communicate it to a wider audience, such as the public or specific communities. This is particularly relevant for missions with a social or community impact.

Practical Steps in Mission Communication

Before proceeding, you'll likely want to create a structured communication plan that outlines how, when, and to whom the mission will be communicated.

In most instances, leadership should be actively involved in communicating the mission. This shows commitment and sets a strong example, and will provide motivation for anyone who might have some initial doubts or concerns.

You probably shouldn't assume you'll be understood the first time, regardless of how clear and direct you try to be in your communications. Consequently, you should encourage feedback and dialogue about the mission, which will reveal how well the mission is actually understood. This feedback will also let you know how well the mission is being received and whether it resonates with the team and stakeholders. You should be prepared to adapt the way the mission is communicated based on the feedback you get, to ensure that you communication remains effective and relevant.

Questions about Communicating the Mission

Given the wide range of topics discussed in this chapter, I have once again broken the questions up by section:

1. Understanding the Importance of Clarity and Simplicity:
  - Why is it important to communicate the mission with clarity and simplicity?

- How does the use of plain language and visual aids enhance the understanding of the mission?

2. Role of Consistency in Mission Communication:
- Why is consistency crucial in communicating the mission?
- How can leaders ensure that the mission is communicated consistently across all platforms?

3. Incorporating Storytelling in Mission Communication:
- What is the significance of incorporating storytelling in communicating the mission?
- Can you provide some examples of how storytelling can make a mission more relatable and engaging?

4. Utilizing Visual and Interactive Elements:
- How do visual and interactive elements enhance the communication of the mission?
- What are some effective visual and interactive methods you could use to convey the mission?

5. Strategies for Implementing Clarity and Simplicity:
- What are some practical steps to implement clarity and simplicity in communicating the mission?
- How can feedback be used to improve the clarity and simplicity of the mission's communication?

6. Achieving Consistency in Mission Communication:
- What are some strategies you can apply to achieve consistency in the communication of the mission?
- What role does leadership play in maintaining this consistency?

7. Storytelling Techniques and Their Impact:

- How can storytelling techniques be used to communicate the mission?

- How does storytelling contribute to the memorability and understanding of the mission?

8. Applying Visual and Interactive Communication:

- What are some examples of visual and interactive elements that can be used in mission communication?

- How can the use of such elements lead to a deeper understanding and engagement with the mission?

9. Understanding the 'Why' of Mission Communication:

- Why is it important to communicate the mission to team members and stakeholders?

- How does communicating the mission guide decision-making and inspire the team?

10. Timing and Audience for Communicating the Mission:

- When is the most effective time to communicate the mission, and why?

- What are the key audiences for mission communication?

- What is the importance of tailoring the message to each group or audience?

11. Developing a Communication Plan:

- What are the key components of an effective communication plan for the mission?

- How can feedback and dialogue be incorporated into this plan to ensure ongoing effectiveness?

Implementing the Mission:
Turning Strategy into Action

The implementation of the mission is the critical juncture where our carefully crafted strategies are tested against the complex realities of the world. This stage is more than just the execution of plans; it represents the translation of our collective vision into tangible outcomes. To navigate this phase effectively, there are several key components we must focus on.

First of all, the delineation of roles and responsibilities is paramount. Each team member must understand not only what their task is, but also how their role fits into the larger puzzle. You'll want to create a clear map of responsibilities so that everyone knows their part and the expectations they'll be facing. This clarity prevents overlap and confusion, ensuring that our efforts are synergistic rather than fragmented.

Exercising leadership is another critical aspect during this phase. Leadership in this context goes beyond merely giving orders or setting the direction. It's also about inspiring confidence and instilling a sense of purpose within the team.

A leader must be the embodiment of the mission's values, demonstrating commitment and resilience. They must be adaptable, capable of making decisive choices in the face of unforeseen challenges, and skilled in juggling the complexities associated with the mission.

Nurturing a cohesive team dynamic is equally essential. The strength of a team lies not just in the skills of individual members, but in how effectively they work together. In my experience, you can create this constructive dynamic by fostering an environment where mutual respect, open communication, and collaboration are all honored and always present. Each team member should feel valued and be encouraged to contribute their unique perspectives, because it is from the melding of diverse ideas and experiences that innovative solutions emerge.

In this chapter, we will explore these components in greater detail, examining how they interact to turn strategic plans into successful missions. We will look at real-world examples where these elements have been effectively employed, and also where they have been neglected. By understanding these dynamics, we can better prepare ourselves to implement missions that are not only strategically sound, but also adaptable and resilient in the face of challenges.

Defining Team Roles and Responsibilities

As you get ready to launch your mission, each team member should have a clear understanding of their role and how it will contribute to the mission's success. This clarity prevents confusion and ensures that every duty or responsibility will be handled by someone.

Ideally, you'll want to assign roles based on individual strengths and skills. This guarantees that each aspect of the mission will fall under the jurisdiction of someone who is competent and confident in that area.

Nevertheless, you should still continuously review and be prepared to adjust roles and responsibilities as the mission progresses, and as team dynamics evolve.

A Clear Definition of Roles: Ensuring Alignment and Efficiency

Defining team roles has always been a cornerstone of success. This will result in each team member understanding not only their responsibilities, but also how their contributions fit into the larger picture.

Importance of Clearly Defined Roles

When roles are clearly defined, team members can focus on specific tasks without uncertainty. This leads to greater efficiency and makes them more effective at completing their work. Clear role definition helps to prevent overlaps in responsibilities, where multiple people end up performing the same task, and it also prevents the persistence of gaps in responsibility that lead to important tasks being overlooked.

Knowing their specific roles, individuals can take ownership and be held accountable for their parts of the mission. This accountability is crucial for both personal and team growth. With clear roles, team members are empowered to make decisions within their realm of responsibility, leading to faster and more effective problem-solving.

Strategies for Defining Roles Clearly

Role definition is a fairly straightforward process. You can start by creating detailed job descriptions that outline not just the tasks that must be completed, but also the expected outcomes, and it can also explain how these outcomes contribute to the overall integrity of the mission.

To further reduce the chances of confusion, you can conduct sessions where team members can discuss and ask for clarification about their roles. This can be particularly helpful in new teams or after a reorganization.

You may also want to establish clear communication channels, where anyone can discuss their roles and responsibilities or address any issues that might arise whenever they would like.

Technology can be utilized effectively in these contexts. You can provide digital tools and resources that facilitate understanding and the efficient monitoring and management of roles, such as project management software or role-mapping diagrams.

The Implementation of Clear Role Definition in Action

At the start of a project, you can outline each team member's role and responsibilities, so that everyone understands how they fit into the bigger picture. You can also conduct regular check-ins or one-on-one sessions to discuss role clarity, address any uncertainties, and make alterations in your practices as necessary. You should always have active feedback mechanisms up and running, so that team members can express concerns or suggest changes regarding their roles.

Matching Skills to Roles: Optimizing Team Effectiveness

Aligning individual skills and strengths with specific roles boosts efficiency, while also unleashing the full potential of each team member. This alignment will play a pivotal role in the successful implementation of the mission, ensuring that every task is approached with the best possible expertise and aptitude.

The Significance of Skill-Role Alignment

By matching skills to roles, each team member can operate in their area of strength, leading to a higher quality of work and greater job satisfaction. When each role is filled by someone with the appropriate skills, the overall team performance is optimized. In every instance, this kind of synergy will lead to more effective and efficient mission implementation.

Aligning skills with roles also allows for adaptability. Team members can grow into their roles more fully over time, acquiring new skills and expanding their expertise. This approach ensures that the team's collective skills are utilized strategically, getting the most out of the available human resources.

Implementing Skill-Role Alignment

To put everyone in the best position to succeed, you'll probably want to perform assessments to understand the skills, strengths, and weaknesses of each team member. Your fact-finding procedures could include formal assessments, interviews, or performance reviews.

In conjunction with this activity you can analyze each role within the mission, to determine exactly what the required skills and competencies might be. This should go beyond basic job descriptions to include any nuances or complications that might arise, any of which could have a bearing on the outcome of the mission.

Your ultimate goal will be to match team members to roles based on the alignment of their skills with the role requirements. You'll likely want to factor in not only technical skills, but also soft skills like communication, leadership, and problem-solving. You should be prepared to adjust roles as new information about team members' skills comes to light, or as the mission evolves.

To further promote a successful result, you can offer training and development opportunities to team members to help them grow into their roles or to develop new skills that dovetail with evolving mission needs. You should always maintain open communication about roles and skills, while encouraging team members to express their interests and career aspirations.

Skill-Role Alignment in Practice

If you aren't entirely sure yet about which abilities your prospective team members do or not possess, you can organize team-building activities that will help reveal their hidden skills and strengths. If roles have already been assigned, you can boost everyone's chances for success by implementing mentorship programs where experienced team members can guide others in developing skills relevant to their positions.

As an additional hedge against anyone feeling overwhelmed or out of their element, you can encourage cross-functional collaboration that will facilitate cooperative efforts. This will allow team members to learn from each other and develop a broader skill set.

Case Study: New Zealand National Rugby Team's New Leadership Encouraged Team-Building Activities.

Once struggling with performance and discipline issues, New Zealand's national rugby team, the All Blacks, underwent a cultural shift under new leadership. The new focus was on building a team with strong character and accountability and a sense of collective responsibility.

Central to this was the concept of "sweeping the sheds," where no individual was bigger than the team, not even star players. This philosophy extended to on-field performance, where every team member's contribution was valued equally.

As might have been predicted, this focus on culture, discipline, and humility translated into remarkable on-field success, making the All Blacks a model of effective team-building under high-quality leadership.

Emphasizing values like humility and teamwork, each player was encouraged to contribute to the team's legacy. This approach led to victory after victory, entrenching the All Blacks as one of the most successful sports teams globally. This illustrates the power of culture and values in building effective teams.

Leadership: Empowering and Guiding

Leaders should empower team members by delegating authority and providing the resources and support needed for everyone to fulfill their roles effectively. Leaders should exemplify the behaviors and attitudes they expect from their team members, since leading by example is a powerful motivator.

As a leader, you should try to maintain open lines of communication and be accessible to team members at all times. This encourages a culture of transparency and trust.

Things You Can Do Today to Cultivate Trust and Cooperation in the Team

Leaders are in a unique position during the pursuit of a mission, having a greater ability to influence team dynamics than anyone else. You will undoubtedly want to use this power responsibly, for the good of your organization and for everyone who works beside you on a daily basis.

Here's a quick glimpse of what responsible leadership looks like:

- Since trust is the foundation of any successful team, you should try to create an environment where honesty, integrity, and mutual respect are fundamental and always on display.

- You can actively encourage the development of a culture of cooperation, where team members support and rely on each other in every way possible. Collaboration over competition can be encouraged within the team.

- You can try to address conflicts promptly and constructively, encouraging open dialogue and seeking mutually beneficial solutions.

- You will enjoy acknowledging and celebrating the achievements of team members, since you know recognition fosters a sense of belonging and appreciation.
- You can conduct regular team-building activities to strengthen relationships and improve team dynamics.

Addressing the Absence of Trust and Cooperation

When it becomes clear to you that trust and cooperation are lacking, you'll want to know why. It could be due to unclear communication, perceived inequities, or lack of alignment with the mission.

Rather than guessing, you can create opportunities for team members to express their concerns and make suggestions. This will promote mutual understanding and help deal with the obstacles that hinder trust and cooperation.

Sometimes leaders may need to intervene directly to address underlying issues. This could involve mediation, revising team structures, or altering communication strategies.

Campaigns Related to the Mission

Every decision and action an organization makes can have far-reaching consequences. In piviotal moments, the importance of well-structured campaigns cannot be overstated.

These campaigns are not just a series of actions, but are strategically designed to reinforce, re-energize, and ultimately achieve the mission. The key lies in staying true to the message, adapting tactics that align with the mission while learning from real-world examples.

Staying on Message

If you want your campaigns to be successful, you should take steps to ensure that every aspect of the campaign consistently reflects the core message and theme. This consistency helps in building recognition and understanding of the mission.

Every message or theme in the campaign, without exception, should be consistent with the mission's values and objectives. This alignment guarantees that the campaign will contribute positively to the accomplishment of the mission.

You'll want to keep the team regularly briefed on the campaign's message and progress, to make sure everyone is onboard and up to speed. This internal coherence is critical for external consistency.

Adapting Tactics to Support the Mission

While the overarching message should remain constant, you'll want to be flexible in the tactics used to convey it. You may have to adapt strategies based on audience response, market changes, or new opportunities. Regardless of how events unfold, you should employ a range of tactics, from digital marketing to community engagement, to funnel everyone back to the central theme of the mission.

Even as your tactics evolve, you should continuously evaluate their effectiveness and be ready to alter them to make sure they contribute to the success of the mission.

Examples of Campaigns in Action

If the mission is to promote sustainable business practices, an awareness campaign could involve educational content, seminars, and partnerships with eco-friendly organizations. In a mission aiming to support a charitable cause, fundraising campaigns can employ tactics like charity events, online crowdfunding, and corporate partnerships to maximize success. For missions aimed at policy change, advocacy campaigns might include lobbying efforts, public rallies, and collaboration with influential policymakers.

Questions about Implementing the Mission

In separate sections, here are some questions that will help you process the amount of information you've been exposed to in this chapter:

1. **Understanding Role Clarity:**
   - Why is having a clear definition of roles important for the successful implementation of a mission?
   - How can regular reviews and adjustments of roles and responsibilities benefit the team's progress towards the mission?

2. **Importance of Skill-Role Alignment:**
   - What is the significance of matching individual skills to specific roles within the team?
   - What are some effective ways to assess and align team members' skills with their roles?

3. **Leadership in Team Building:**
   - How does empowering team members and serving as a role model contribute to effective leadership?
   - What strategies can leaders use to cultivate trust and cooperation within the team?

4. **Addressing Lack of Trust and Cooperation:**
   - What are some possible root causes of an absence of trust and cooperation in a team?
   - How can open forums and leadership interventions help in addressing these issues?

5. **Role of Leadership in Mission Implementation:**
   - Can you explain the role of leadership in guiding and empowering team members during the implementation of a mission?

- What qualities should leaders exhibit to effectively steer the team towards achieving the mission?

6. Strategies for Defining Team Roles Clearly:
- What strategies can be employed to ensure that team roles are clearly defined and understood?
- How can role clarification sessions and regular feedback help in maintaining role clarity?

7. Maximizing Team Performance through Skill Alignment:
- How does aligning team members' skills with their roles optimize overall team performance?
- What is the importance of adaptability and learning in the context of skill-role alignment?

8. Case Study Analysis - New Zealand Rugby Team:
- What cultural shifts and leadership strategies were employed by the New Zealand Rugby Team to enhance team performance?
- How did the concept of "sweeping the sheds" contribute to building a successful team dynamic?

9. Cultivating Trust and Cooperation:
- What methods can be used to build trust and encourage cooperation within a team?
- How can regular team-building activities and acknowledgment of contributions enhance team dynamics?

10. Overcoming Challenges in Team Dynamics:
- What are some of the strategies you can use to overcome challenges related to trust and cooperation in a team?
- What role does open communication play in resolving conflicts and fostering a positive team environment?

The Next Mission: Fostering Evolution and Growth

Over the course of my 25-year career, I've seen time and again how the concept of the Next Mission can have a constructive impact in various contexts. It can help resolve critical conflicts, empower the creation of high-level corporate strategies, and a whole lot more. This idea goes beyond the simple notion of moving from one task to another. In reality, it represents an evolutionary leap for both the team and the entire mission cycle.

This evolutionary step encapsulates the vital processes of learning and growth. It creates a dynamic where team members acquire new skills as they deepen their understanding of their successes and the reasons for them. This understanding is not limited to the task at hand, but extends to the broader context in which we operate. It's about grasping the underlying principles that guarantee achievement in all of our endeavors.

Moreover, this step is grounded in adaptation. In a world that's constantly changing, the ability to adapt is not only invaluable, it's imperative. Focusing on the Next Mission requires us to analyze past successes and failures, to understand what worked and what didn't, and why. This analysis then informs how we approach new challenges, ensuring that we're not just reacting to changes but actively anticipating and preparing for them.

Thinking about the Next Mission also opens up opportunities that might have been previously unseen. It encourages us to look at situations through a fresh lens, to seek out new possibilities, and to be bold in our aspirations. It rejects the acceptance of the status quo in favor of continually striving for excellence and innovation.

In essence, the Next Mission is a mindset. It's an ethos that drives continuous improvement and the relentless pursuit of success. It's what separates good teams from great ones, and solid strategies from transformative ones.

As we close this chapter, and indeed this book, I urge you to embrace the concept of the Next Mission. You should see it not just as a necessary step, but as an opportunity to grow, to lead, and to excel in whatever challenges you face in the future.

Evolving the Team

The next mission should be informed by the lessons learned from previous endeavors. This involves analyzing successes and shortcomings to understand what can be improved.

Based on what you learn, you can sharpen your focus and increase your effectiveness in developing the team's skills. You might experiment with training in new technologies or leadership development, or sponsor workshops for your team that concentrate on emerging industry trends.

Sometimes, evolving the team may mean changing its composition. You may sometimes need to bring in new people with skills and talents that are more aligned with the upcoming mission's needs. You should also continue your efforts to create a culture where team members are encouraged to introduce new ideas or propose innovative solutions. This mindset will be crucial for the evolving challenges of the next mission.

Growing the Cycle

As you explore the Next Mission concept, you can use the momentum and achievements of the previous mission to propel you on to the next. This could involve expanding on a successful strategy or leveraging established relationships.

Based on what you've learned, you may want to consider broadening the scope of the next mission. This could mean tackling more complex problems, reaching out to new markets, or addressing issues on a larger scale.

With an emphasis on growth, you can focus on how the next mission can contribute to the long-term sustainability and expansion of the organization. This foresight is critical in ensuring the ongoing relevance and impact of your work.

You can try to incorporate the concept of continuous improvement into the team's culture. You may be able to do this through regular reviews, feedback, and a proactive approach to seeking better ways to get things done.

Examples of Next Missions

If a particular project is successful, the next mission could be to develop it into a broader program with wider objectives and a larger impact. For a business, the next mission could involve taking a successful product or service to new geographical markets or different customer segments.

In a mission that achieves policy change at a local level, the next mission might aim to influence policy at a national or even international level.

This is an intriguing and fascinating way to look at things. It prevents organizational complacency, which can prevent you from accomplishing any mission if you allow it to set in.

Some Parting Notes

As we conclude From War Zones to Boardrooms: Optimize the Moment When Strategic Planning Fails, I pay tribute to those who have courageously faced pivotal moments without flinching, leading with purpose and resilience. Their stories inspire and motivate me, reminding us all of the profound impact of the moments that fulfill our purpose, often realized in hindsight. Our world, ever turbulent, demands we think differently, reevaluate our decisions, and approach challenges with a fresh perspective, if we want to get ahead and help others do the same.

This book is designed to provoke discussion, heighten awareness of critical moments, and challenge the status quo in both the business and personal spheres. It's a call to recognize that a mission focused solely on profit lacks depth and sustainability.

True missions should encompass more than transactional goals; they should reflect an awareness of a company's reputation, customer values, and societal impact. Optimize the Moment is my bold statement to leaders, urging them to redefine success and lead with a vision that transcends the conventional.

I extend a personal call to action. It's time for us all to harness the lessons of adaptability, resilience, and conscientious decision-making. We should reflect on the varied experiences and insights we share, recognizing the power within each moment to make a difference. We should all embrace the inevitability of change, seize emerging opportunities with boldness, and commit to lifelong learning and improvement.

I suggest you let this book be your guide in transforming challenges into opportunities for growth and success. Your journey to mastering the art of optimizing each moment begins now. Take this knowledge, apply it in your professional and personal life, and let's all learn to embody the changes we wish to see.

Acknowledgments

This book spans the past 25 years of my experiences and as such, there are so many people who have influenced me, inspired me, and challenged me in a variety of ways. Several have taught me how to learn and how to be a better student of the world around us. They've educated me about human behaviour and about the importance of always striving to be a better person.

I am not the first parent who looks into the eyes of their children with a combination of unconditional love, overwhelming pride, and a dose of trepidation about the world into which we have brought them. I am beyond grateful for the daily gifts both Emily and Adam continue to give, not only to me but to everyone around them, as they find their own paths and demonstrate their kindness, generosity, empathy, and grasp of the "Moments" in their own ways. They continue to teach me so much.

Thanks to my remarkable parents, who planted in me the seeds of desire to read, learn, travel, explore, and above all, to embrace the notion of service to others as a cause that is far more important than material things or personal ambitions. My father, Malcolm Rust, and my stepmother Donna, in St. Thomas, Ontario., for over forty years have been a rock of stability and sanity for me in an often chaotic and fluid world. Along with stepsister Dayna (December 1992), stepbrothers Ryan and Todd, and in-law Kelly, they have provided a home base, a lot of laughs, and a heart-warming family offering support through thick and thin. They have put up with all my crazy ideas and my whims without question, for which I will be forever grateful.

I must also say thanks to my mother, Marjorie Rust, who died on February 26, 2010 after a decade-long battle with Alzheimer's and dementia. I miss her every single day and deeply regret the nature of the illness that tortured her during her last days and slowly, painfully, took the joy from her life. I knew her to be highly intelligent, principled, kind, and caring ... and full of mischief! Her love of books started at an early age and although very uncommon for a country girl growing up in rural Yorkshire, UK in the 1930s, she went to university in Leeds and became the Children's Librarian in Lincoln. She taught us a love of books and learning, and a discipline for schooling and a work ethic that served my brother and me well later in life. I often think of those foundational skills she instilled in us, those key critical thinking capacities, even though we didn't call them that at the time. Her influence is undeniable, and I so wish she were alive to see this book published.

My brother, Andrew, sister-in-law Joanne, their kids, Spencer (Allie), Carlyn (Katie), Meghan (Chris), live in the Ottawa area and have also provided a stable home base during times of chaos and uncertainty in my life, for which I am so grateful. Sharing "Moments" with family is one of life's gifts and watching our children grow, find their paths, love, have their own kids, and explore the world has been special, and a true reminder of how precious our time here really is.

Amanda Smith has a title of "Business Manager," but that is simply not adequate to describe Amanda's role in my life or in the creation of this book. Amanda has been an absolute blessing, a constant, and an unrelenting voice of support and encouragement through all the ups and downs these past seven years. She has worked tirelessly to help keep the wheels on and to keep me out of trouble. Always professional, always kind, thoughtful, and knowledgeable, I simply don't know where I would be without her.

Jeffrey Kroeker, thank you for kindly providing such a thoughtful foreword for the book. I truly valued our shared experiences and our time together overseas. Our friendship has only grown over the years, and I have learned so much from you. You are a force, and your clients only benefit from your channeling of all that knowledge and energy.

Jaime Watt, Executive Chair of Navigator Ltd., in Toronto. Jaime has been a close friend, a mentor, an inspiration, and a colleague for over 25 years. Many of the experiences I have had simply wouldn't have been possible unless Jaime had opened the door, made the introduction, or encouraged me to pursue something. He has a gift that way. He has motivated me, provided opportunities, challenged me, employed me, let me sleep on his couch, and in countless other ways supported me over the years. With his partner, Paul, they have been like family to me and my kids and have shared good times and heartaches. I simply cannot express my gratitude for Jaime's influence on my thinking and my life, and for the many experiences we have shared.

Lisa Samson, Partner, StrategyCorp, Ottawa, Ontario. Lisa has been a business partner and close friend for over a decade, and I am truly grateful to Lisa for the opportunity to work together and to learn from her, and for the flexibility she has given me to do my own thing these past few years. Lisa demonstrates on a daily basis leadership through kindness, empathy, and "mission" innately, and has built a purpose-driven team of talented individuals who jump out of bed every day wanting to be part of the cause. Most of all, I am profoundly grateful for Lisa's friendship and support these past few years. Her quiet sense of conviction and strong moral compass is her "superpower," and it is reflected every day in what she does.

A special note of gratitude for my Pinewood Stables family, Mara Frew and the group of people who share my passion and love of horses, but who have become so much more. As you put the "mission" of every horse's health and well-being first, you also embrace and support each other in ways I never imagined. Horses teach us about empathy, confidence, love, influence, and so many other things. All of you have demonstrated the strength and resilience of a team with a sense of belonging. I feel so blessed for all of the "moments" we have had together.

A word of appreciation for the National Democratic Institute and the International Republican Institute, two remarkable organizations dedicated to safeguarding and supporting democracy. In a world where it seems that democracy, as we know it, is at risk, the individuals who take up the call for these organizations, from around the globe, are truly driven by a cause greater than themselves. We rarely ever know of their efforts or their achievements, but I know that they are impactful, meaningful, and so very important, and I want to thank them for their service on behalf of us all. It is not an overstatement to say the world is a better place because of what they do.

This project would not have come to life without Sarah Ratliff, Editor Extraordinaire! Sarah has worked with me to take my writings, my notes, my words, stories, ramblings, and at times, passionate rants, and turn them into something I am hoping is somewhat coherent. It has been a process, and I am so grateful to Sarah for her patience, insights, and positivity.

I want to thank Sanja Dzadzevic for the design and layout of the book. I have learned a lot about the process and have been blessed to have access to the expertise and knowledge of such gifted people as Sanja!

About the Author

Photo by Lindsey Gibeau

Martin Rust is a consultant, working with governmental agencies in Canada and Fortune 100 companies. His practical approach to delivering outcomes leans on over two decades of experience gathering intelligence, analyzing data points, and objectively determining the best path forward. He is known for problem-solving, negotiation skills, conflict resolution, and powerful messaging development.

www.ingramcontent.com/pod-product-compliance
Lightning Source LLC
Chambersburg PA
CBHW070059030426

42335CB00016B/1951